ITALY

MEDITERRANEAN CUISINE

ITALY

MEDITERRANEAN CUISINE

KÖNEMANN

Contents

List of Recipes

Fish & Seafood 88

Meat & Poultry 124

Desserts & Pastries 152

Hot & Cold
Appetizers

Vegetable

Preparation time:	*35 minutes*
Marinating:	*20 minutes*
Cooking time:	*45 minutes*
Difficulty:	☆

Serves 4

2	red bell peppers
	coarse salt
2 tbsp	olive oil
2	eggplants
2	zucchini

For the dressing:

4 tbsp	balsamic vinegar
4 tbsp	olive oil

	salt
	pepper

For the marinade:

	salt
	peppercorns
7 tbsp	olive oil
12	fresh mint leaves
1 tsp	bouquet garni

For the garnish:

	parmesan shavings
	arugula leaves
	cherry tomatoes

Italian cuisine has an endless range of antipasti, which are served as light appetizers. The vegetable dish that we have devised for you in this recipe is easy to prepare – a classic in Italian cookery.

The Italian peninsula is a unique vegetable garden, in which eggplants, zucchini, peppers, tomatoes, and many other types of vegetable flourish. Stroll around the markets and, wherever you go, you will find stalls with beautifully arranged displays and wonderful combinations of colors and aromas. Watch discriminating Italian housewives as they take time to choose the best produce for their families.

Zucchini and eggplants are quintessential summer vegetables and are therefore found in many Mediterranean recipes; here, they are sliced thinly and broiled, then marinated for about 20 minutes in olive oil and seasoned with mint leaves. Mint is rich in calcium, iron, and vitamins and is said to have remarkable stimulant properties. There are dozens of varieties of this plant, the best known of which is the green mint with long, toothed leaves. It is available all year round and will stay fresh for a reasonable time if kept in plastic wrap in the refrigerator.

The marinade is enhanced with a bouquet garni. This mixture of herbs generally includes bay, rosemary, thyme, and savory and is often used when broiling. As a final touch to this antipasto dish, our chef adds arugula, with its characteristic sharp flavor reminiscent of filberts.

This delicious cold appetizer evokes the finest hot summer days in the Italian countryside.

Lay the peppers on a baking sheet. Sprinkle with a generous pinch of salt and pour over 1 tbsp olive oil. Bake for about 45 minutes, skin the peppers, then remove the seeds and cut into thin strips.

Wash the eggplants and zucchini and cut them into thin, even slices.

Pour the remaining oil into a broiler pan and broil the eggplant and zucchini.

Antipasti

Lay the broiled vegetables in an oven-proof dish. Season with salt and crushed peppercorns. Drizzle over the olive oil with mint and bouquet garni herbs and marinate for 20 minutes.

For the dressing, put the balsamic vinegar, olive oil, and salt and pepper in a small dish and beat well with a balloon whisk.

Shave small rolls of parmesan from a block. Arrange the zucchini and eggplant slices with the strips of pepper on a plate. Pour the dressing over the vegetables. Garnish with a few arugula leaves, cherry tomatoes, and parmesan shavings.

Antipasto

Preparation time: 10 minutes
Cooking time: 15 minutes
Difficulty: ★

Serves 4

8 oz/200 g   sole
8 oz/200 g   small squid
6 oz/150 g   Venus clams
⅔ pint/400 g   small langoustines

4   small fresh shrimp
4   large fresh shrimp
½   lemon
                    salt
2 tbsp   olive oil
½ bunch   parsley

In Italy, a main course of fish is traditionally preceded by a seafood salad. This *antipasto alla Giuliese* is one of the culinary classics of the Italian peninsula.

It is especially popular in Giulianova, a friendly little fishing port on the Adriatic coast. The sea in this region has an incredibly wide variety of fish, and the people who live here are great seafood devotees.

This appetizer can be eaten either hot or cold and is very easy to prepare. We season the seafood with olive oil, parsley, and salt, but mayonnaise can be used instead just as successfully.

In the regional dialect, the small langoustines that are found in abundance in the Adriatic are called *scampetti piccoli*. They look like lobsters or large shrimp and taste wonderful. They are excellent in salads, but are also occasionally poached or broiled. You can find them at the fishmonger's all the year round, alive or deep-frozen. When you buy them, make sure that the eyes and claws are shiny. Langoustines are only cooked very briefly. One or two langoustines complete with their heads look extremely decorative when arranged on each plate.

In addition to the large and small shrimp, we use small squid in this recipe, but cuttlefish (sepia), a relative of the squid, can be substituted. The flesh of small squid is particularly succulent.

The flesh of the sole, majestic among the flatfish, is delicate and complements the abundant flavors in this appetizer.

Gut the sole and remove the skin. Poach for 5 minutes in salted water. Prepare and wash the squid. Cut into small cubes. Simmer for about 10 minutes in a pan of water.

Place the Venus clams in a pan with some water, cover and cook for a few minutes until the shells have opened. Remove the meat.

Peel the langoustines and shrimp. Cook separately in water for about 3 minutes.

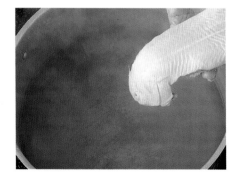

alla Giuliese

Separate the sole fillets using a knife and fork and cut into small, even-sized pieces.

Transfer the langoustines, shrimp, diced squid, Venus clams, and sole to a salad bowl.

For the dressing, squeeze the half lemon and mix the juice in a small bowl with salt, olive oil, and chopped parsley. Serve the seafood with the dressing poured over it.

Artichokes

Preparation time:	20 minutes
Cooking time:	20 minutes
Difficulty:	☆

Serves 4

8	artichokes
1	lemon
1 bunch	fresh mint
2 bunches	parsley

2 cloves	garlic
	salt
8 tbsp	olive oil
scant ½ cup/	
100 ml	white wine

For the garnish:

	fresh fava beans
	pecorino shavings

This artichoke dish, which can be served warm or hot, is a classic in Italian cuisine and is very popular at Easter time. A Roman specialty, it is very easy to prepare. In addition to the numerous varieties of artichoke native to Rome and its environs, the vegetable stalls in the "eternal city" also offer regional variations such as the thick *Romanesco*, which is quite round in shape and thornless, the *Catanese* with its spindle-shaped leaves, the *Violetto* from Tuscany and the area around Palermo, small Ligurian artichokes, and many others besides.

Buy the youngest possible artichokes, which are recognizable by their pretty green and purple color and are so tender that you can eat them raw. Make sure that the leaves are neither damaged nor marked, and that the flower head is still tightly closed. Place the artichokes in water with a dash of lemon juice to prevent discoloration, then drain.

Long ago, the ancient Romans set great store by artichokes, which originate from Sicily. They named them *cynara*, for a young girl in ancient Roman folklore who gradually turned into an artichoke. The Italians then named the plant *carciofo*, from the Arabic *kharsufa*. During the Renaissance, scholars believed the artichoke possessed therapeutic powers. Bartolomeo Scappi, the personal chef of Pope Pius V, recommended stuffing the head of this thistlelike plant with lean veal, ham, eggs, spices, garlic, and aromatic herbs.

The Romans opted for a lighter version. In addition to garlic and parsley – extremely common flavorings in Italy – this filling contains mint, the fresh, powerful flavor of which goes outstandingly well with artichokes. Prepared in this way, artichokes are a delight for gourmets everywhere.

Remove the fibrous outer leaves of the artichokes. Cut off the stalk crossways at the bottom and peel.

Cut off the top leaves horizontally. Open out the artichokes and place in a bowl of water containing lemon juice.

Wash and chop the mint and parsley. Peel the garlic cloves and chop finely. Stuff the artichokes with this mixture.

Roman Style

Carefully dip the tips of the artichokes in a dish of salt.

Hold the artichokes by the stalk and place them in a saucepan. Pour over 8 tbsp olive oil. Cover and simmer for 3 minutes.

Pour in the white wine. Cover, turn up the heat, and bring to the boil, then simmer for approximately 15 minutes over low heat. Serve the artichokes garnished with fava beans and pecorino shavings.

Deep-fried

Preparation time:	30 minutes
Cooking time:	15 minutes
Difficulty:	✶

Serves 4

8 oz/200 g	small cuttlefish
20	langoustines
20	fresh shrimp
2 cups/250 g	flour
	oil for frying
	salt

For the sauce tartare:

2	egg yolks
	salt

	pepper
¾ cup+1 tbsp/	
200 ml	sunflower oil
2 tbsp	capers
5 sprigs	parsley
3	gherkins

For the garnish:

	basil leaves

To serve:

	lemons

The gulf of Naples is world-famous, not only for its beauty, but also for its fishing grounds. The Mediterranean Sea, known in ancient times as *Mare nostrum*, or "our sea," has been supplying the inhabitants of southern Italy with fish, mussels, and crustaceans since time immemorial.

Our deep-fried seafood is quick and easy to prepare. Depending on availability, red mullet or red snapper, anchovies, and sardines can also be used for this recipe.

Langoustines are found in abundance in western European coastal waters. They have very tasty flesh, reminiscent of lobster, and are excellent for broiling or poaching. They are also very good in most recipes featuring crustaceans, and are served with the pincers left on. They are available all year round.

Fresh shrimp are highly prized by connoisseurs for their extremely fine flavor.

Small cuttlefish, related to squid (*calamari*), have succulent, delicate flesh. They can be broiled, fried, or stuffed. Around 20 inches/50 centimeters in length, they have spiral-shaped bodies, dark-colored skin, and two triangular fins at the tail end. There are ten edible tentacles at the head end, two of which are very long.

To enhance our seafood recipe, the chef suggests serving sauce tartare, which has the subtle flavor of capers. The flower buds of the caper bush are harvested in spring. Since capers are preserved in vinegar or brine, they need thorough rinsing before use. In Italy, capers from Lipari and Pantelleria, islands off the coast of Sicily, are especially popular.

Clean the cuttlefish under running water. Carefully remove the head and tentacles, then remove the ink sac and quill. Cut the flesh into even-sized pieces.

Remove the heads from the langoustines and shrimp by giving a slight twist, then peel the tails.

Place the flour in a large dish. Dip the cuttlefish, langoustines, and shrimp in the flour and carefully shake off any excess.

Seafood

Heat the oil and add the cuttlefish, langoustines, and shrimp. Deep-fry the basil leaves (for the garnish) with the seafood.

Remove the cuttlefish, langoustines, and shrimp from the oil, drain on paper towels, and season generously with salt.

Sauce tartare: Mix the egg yolks, salt, and pepper into a creamy sauce. Then, beating constantly, add the oil a little at a time. Stir in the capers, chopped parsley, and diced gherkins. Serve the deep-fried seafood with the sauce and slices of lemon. Garnish with basil.

Liver Guazzetto with

Soaking time:	*overnight*
Preparation time:	*15 minutes*
Cooking time:	*40 minutes*
Difficulty:	✳

Serves 4

For the guazzetto:

¾ oz/20 g	dried porcini mushrooms
8 tbsp	extra-virgin olive oil
½ clove	garlic
½ bunch	parsley

	salt
	pepper
4	chicken livers
1	onion

For the polenta:

1 scant cup/	
150 g	cornmeal
	salt

For the garnish:

	parsley
	chives

Guazzetto was once a dish that was eaten mainly by the poor. When a chicken was killed, they naturally could not afford to throw anything away; the liver was therefore used to make a *guazzetto* and the skin was cut into strips and made into a kind of *fettucini*.

In the mushroom season, fresh porcini mushrooms (of which there are several sub-species) should be used if possible. Out of season, dried mushrooms can be used instead; these have to be washed thoroughly and soaked in cold water. Biancarosa Zecchin suggests serving the mixture of liver, onions, and fried porcini mushrooms on a bed of polenta.

Polenta has played a major role in the cuisine of northern Italy for several centuries. Corn was introduced from America by Venetian merchants in the 16th century, and the thick broth prepared from cornmeal, like those previously made from barley, millet, spelt, and garbanzo beans, became very popular very soon afterward. Corn, which was a staple food for poor peasant farmers in particular, did a great deal to relieve famines, and eventually cornmeal broth could be found on the table at any time of the day. This extremely restricted diet did, however, result in serious malnutrition.

The classic cornmeal broth for polenta has to be stirred for 45–60 minutes on the stove. We therefore recommend pre-cooked polenta, which is easier to prepare. It is cooked over low heat until it reaches the consistency of oatmeal porridge. It can also be cooked for longer and then poured into a dish; after it has cooled, it can then be turned out and served cut into slices.

Guazzetto is a delicious appetizer, but can also be served as a main course.

Soak the dried porcini mushrooms in lukewarm water for 20 minutes. For the polenta, bring 4 cups/1 l water to the boil in a saucepan and add the cornmeal and salt. Stir for about 20 minutes until the consistency of oatmeal porridge is reached. Set aside.

For the guazzetto, drain the mushrooms and chop with a knife.

Heat 4 tbsp olive oil in a pan and sauté the mushrooms with the chopped garlic, chopped parsley, salt, and pepper for about 5 minutes.

Porcini Mushrooms

Cut the chicken livers into strips.

Peel and chop the onion. Heat the remaining olive oil in another pan and sauté the onion. Add the livers, then season with salt and pepper. Stir with a spoon for 3–4 minutes until browned.

Add the browned livers to the mushrooms. Fry for another 4–5 minutes, stirring constantly. Serve the livers with the porcini mushrooms on a bed of polenta, and sprinkle with chopped parsley and chives.

Gratin of Mussels

Preparation time:	25 minutes
Cooking time:	15 minutes
Difficulty:	★

Serves 4

7 lb/3 kg	mussels
4	large tomatoes
1 clove	garlic
1 bunch	parsley

6 tbsp	olive oil
	breadcrumbs to bind
	salt

For the garnish:

	parsley

Today it is almost impossible to imagine Italian cuisine without tomatoes – *pomodori* in Italian – and the bright red tomatoes make this gratin of mussels look particularly appealing. The mussels are easy to prepare and excellent when served as a light appetizer among friends.

Mussels are very delicate and must be eaten within three days of being harvested. Choose them very carefully and avoid those that have broken shells or are slightly open. Fresh mussels are always tightly closed. Before cooking, they must be cleaned by removing the beards and then scrubbing them under running water. The chef suggests substituting Venus clams, with their particularly delicate and flavorsome flesh, for the mussels if necessary. The filling contains garlic, giving the recipe a Mediterranean feel. Garlic has been cultivated for over 5,000 years and is absolutely indispensable in the cuisine of southern Europe.

Parsley goes wonderfully well with garlic, and can be bought all year round. In Italy, people who are held in universally high esteem are described as *come il prezzemolo*, as essential as parsley in the kitchen.

Tomatoes are a staple ingredient in Mediterranean cuisine. Although the conquistadors had brought the tomato to Europe from Peru, it was only in the 18th century that it was cultivated in Campagna. At that time it was called *pomo d'oro* ("golden apple") because of its yellow color. Today, tomatoes are eaten all year round. There are around 5,000 known varieties, including the famous *Roma*, originally from the southern part of the country. Choose firm, fleshy tomatoes with a uniform, brilliant red color.

Clean the mussels and remove the beards with the tip of a knife. Place in a saucepan with water and boil for 3–5 minutes until they open.

Leave the mussels to cool and remove the meat from the shells. Set aside. Blanch and skin the tomatoes, remove the seeds, and dice into small cubes.

For the filling, peel and chop the clove of garlic. Wash the parsley and chop.

with Tomatoes

Transfer the mussel meat with the parsley and garlic to a bowl and pour 2 tbsp olive oil over the top. Add the breadcrumbs. Season with salt and mix carefully.

When the mussels are completely coated, fill the mussel shells with the breadcrumb/meat mixture and press it down lightly.

Lay the filled shells in a ovenproof dish. Scatter the diced tomatoes on top. Season with salt and pour the remaining olive oil and 4–5 tbsp/60–75 ml water over the top. Bake at 350° F/180 °C for 10 minutes. Serve the mussels garnished with parsley.

Baked Eggplants

Preparation time:	*40 minutes*
Cooking time:	*2 hours 20 minutes*
Difficulty:	✫

Serves 4

3	carrots
2	onions
1 clove	garlic
1 stick	celery
4 tbsp	olive oil

4 tbsp	white wine
1¾ lb/800 g	tomatoes
	salt
8	eggplants
2	buffalo mozzarella cheeses
	oil for frying
3½ tbsp/50g	grated parmesan
1 bunch	basil

For the garnish:

	basil leaves

Baked eggplants with parmesan is a classic dish. It is easy to prepare and there are many local variations. In Sicily, for example, it is served with grated chocolate, while the Neapolitans add sweetbreads.

The flavorsome vegetarian recipe here, in which the eggplant slices are strewn liberally with parmesan cheese before being placed in a hot broiler, is originally from Calabria. In Italian it is called *parmigiana di melanzane*, taking its name from the famous cheese that comes from northern Italy.

The eggplant, a classic summer vegetable, was probably introduced into southern Italy by the Arabs, who called it *badindshan*. A dry climate, silicon-rich soil, and high temperatures are essential for the successful cultivation of eggplants. These three factors prevent bitter substances forming in the flesh of the vegetable and provide favorable conditions for the concentrated, yet mild, flavor to develop. There are a number of varieties, distinguished by their different shape and color.

The various kinds are found in abundance in Italian markets between October and June – *Violetta di Firenze*, *Belleza nera*, and *Nubia*, for example. When buying them, make sure that the stalks are still intact, the skins are smooth and unmarked, and the flesh is undamaged and firm: in other words, that they are as fresh as possible. Eggplants keep well in the refrigerator.

Parmesan is the typical ingredient in this recipe. True parmesan can only be produced in the provinces of Parma, Reggio-Emilia, Modena, Mantua, and Bologna, where it is still made by hand. Its flavor is unmistakable: highly salted and sometimes sharp.

Peel the carrots, onions, and the garlic clove. Cut the celery and carrots into sticks and slice the onions. Crush the garlic.

Heat the olive oil. Add the carrots, onions, celery, and garlic and sauté for 15 minutes over a low heat. Pour in the white wine and reduce.

Blanch and skin the tomatoes, then add to the vegetables in the saucepan. Cover and simmer for about 1 hour. Season with salt to taste.

with Cheese

Wash the eggplants and cut into even-sized, thick slices. Slice the mozzarella cheeses.

Heat the oil in a skillet and add the eggplant slices. Deep-fry until they are golden brown, remove, and drain on paper towels.

Pour the vegetable mixture into an oven-proof dish. Arrange a layer of eggplant slices on top and sprinkle with parmesan. Layer the mozzarella and basil on the eggplant and repeat, ending with a layer of eggplant. Bake at 350° F/180° C for 1 hour. Garnish with basil before serving.

Bread Soup

Preparation time:	15 minutes
Cooking time:	20 minutes
Difficulty:	☆

Serves 4

1¼ lb/500 g	broccoli
4 tbsp	olive oil
2 cloves	garlic
1	dried chile
1	mild dried red chile

	salt
	pepper
8 oz/200 g	stale bread
2 oz/50 g	pecorino cheese
	coarse salt

This bread soup is typical of the countryside around Naples. This dish, which unquestionably originated in poor farmhouse kitchens, can be served as a light main course or as an appetizer. In some families, the soup is also made with potatoes, eggs, and winter endive. The list of ingredients was once much more modest than this, consisting only of stale bread supplemented with different vegetables from the garden.

Broccoli is grown mainly in southern Italy. It belongs to the brassica family and is rich in vitamin C and minerals. Its relative, cauliflower, can be substituted for broccoli in this recipe. Broccoli is available from October to April. When preparing the soup, reserve the water in which the broccoli has been cooked and soak the bread in it.

Italian olive oil does not always taste the same; it can be mild or very strong, with varying degrees of fruitiness. Oil from Apulia, for instance, has a sharp flavor. The olives are harvested between the beginning of November and mid-December, and are still gathered by hand today. The workers draw special rakes through the foliage, with the fruits falling onto nylon sheets or nets spread out under the trees before being transported to the mill. After the leaves and stalks have been removed, the olives are washed and crushed. The ensuing pulp is then carefully stirred, with layers of around 1 inch/2 centimeters in thickness then being pressed hydraulically. The oil is separated from the emergent liquid with a centrifuge. The freshly pressed oil is stored in earthenware jugs, protected from light and temperature fluctuations, and takes 30–40 days to clear, after which it is filtered again. Choose extra-virgin olive oil from the first pressing, as our chef has done.

Separate the broccoli florets from the stalk and cook for 10 minutes in boiling salted water. Remove and drain. Reserve the water for soaking the bread.

Place a dozen ice cubes in a salad bowl and cover with water, add the broccoli and leave to cool for a few minutes, then drain.

Heat the olive oil in a pan and sauté the chopped garlic and chiles. Add the broccoli and cook for 5 minutes, then season with salt and pepper.

with Broccoli

Cut the bread into large, even-sized cubes.

Soak the bread for a few minutes in the water in which the broccoli was cooked.

Add the bread to the broccoli in the pan. Pour in a little of the water and squash the bread down. Leave for a few minutes in the pan to infuse. Serve and sprinkle with grated pecorino and coarse salt to taste.

Friulian

Preparation time: 20 minutes
Cooking time: 18 minutes
Difficulty: ★

Serves 4

4	eggs
12 oz/300 g	lamb's lettuce
6 oz/150 g	pancetta (or other smoked slab bacon)
3 tbsp	extra-virgin olive oil
2 tbsp	balsamic vinegar

1	salt pomegranate

In his restaurant in Cormons, between Gorizia and Udine in Friuli, chef Paolo Zoppolatti serves his guests a fresh lamb's lettuce salad with eggs and pancetta. He has adapted this traditional recipe to suit modern tastes, separating the yolks and whites of the hard-boiled eggs, slicing the whites and passing the yolks through a sieve, and sprinkling pomegranate seeds over the finished dish.

Buy only fresh, brilliant green lamb's lettuce for this recipe. Lamb's lettuce is a delicate fall and winter vegetable that grows well on sandy soil. Even in its original packaging, it will keep no longer than three or four days in the refrigerator. It should be washed briefly under running water and then left to drain – but not dried. Endive or dandelion can be added to the lamb's lettuce in this recipe.

The charm of this Friulian salad lies in the richly contrasting flavors, ranging from the salty, smoky flavor of the bacon and the acidity of the vinegar through the sweetness of the pomegranate seeds. Although the bacon used in Friuli is first peppered and then either smoked for 12 hours or dried in the cellar for 12 days, ordinary strips of bacon or smoked ham can also be used.

The balsamic vinegar comes from Modena in Emilia-Romagna. It is made from the must of white grapes and is matured in casks for several years. During this time, it is transferred several times to casks made from different kinds of wood. According to connoisseurs, it takes 12 years to achieve perfection. Its sweet-sour character goes wonderfully well with this salad.

Hard-boil the eggs. Wash the lamb's lettuce, drain, and then remove the tiny roots at the base of the leaves.

Leave the eggs to cool and then remove the shells. Remove the yolks with a small spoon and pass through a sieve. Cut the egg white into slices.

Cut the pancetta or bacon into cubes.

Salad

Fry the pancetta cubes in the olive oil in a skillet for 5 minutes, turning frequently.

When the bacon is well done, quench with the balsamic vinegar and season with salt. Fry for another 2 or 3 minutes over a hot flame, while shaking the skillet vigorously.

Cut the pomegranate into quarters and carefully remove the seeds. Place the lamb's lettuce in the middle of a plate and arrange the egg white all around it, then top with the egg yolk, pancetta, pomegranate seeds, and the liquor from the skillet.

Fennel Salad

Preparation time: 15 minutes
Cooking time: 20 minutes
Difficulty: *

Serves 4

2	fennel bulbs
6 tbsp	olive oil
	salt
	pepper
4	oranges
12	black olives

For the garnish:

fennel seeds
fennel leaves

This fennel salad with oranges, highly regarded by gourmets from Rome to Palermo, is very refreshing and provides a real vitamin boost. It is also very easy to prepare. Fennel grows wild in southern Italy; today, it is cultivated in Apulia and exported all over the world. This aromatic plant, which has a high calcium content, flourishes in the sandy soils around the Mediterranean. It can grow up to 6 feet/2 meters tall, has feathery, dark green foliage, and smells a little like aniseed. It has been eaten since time immemorial as a vegetable, but has also been used for medicinal purposes.

Fennel is sold practically everywhere during the winter. Choose small bulbs that are tender, white, and firm. The fluffy little shoots at the end of the stalks should not be thrown away, because they add flavor to the sauce.

The oranges are a reminder of southern Italy and Sicily, an island that was providing high-quality citrus fruit as far back as the Middle Ages. The Arabian writer, Ibn Zaffir, sang the praises of the orange and lemon trees in the gardens of Palermo: "In Sicily, the trees have fiery heads and stand with their feet in the water." The first orange trees were probably introduced in the 11th or 12th century. Monks subsequently cultivated a number of different varieties of orange on the Palermo plain, which has since been known as the *Conca d'oro*. Seventy percent of Italian oranges still come from Sicily.

For this salad, we recommend either the famous navel oranges or blood oranges, which are very juicy.

Remove the outer layers from the fennel, then cut off the base of each bulb.

Cut the fennel bulbs into even-sized, small cubes. Chop the fennel leaves.

To make the marinade, pour the olive oil into a salad bowl and season with salt and pepper. Add the cubed fennel and fennel leaves and infuse for 20 minutes. Stir gently.

with Oranges

Remove all the peel from the oranges.

Cut the oranges crossways into even slices. Capture and reserve the juice.

Pit the olives. Arrange the fennel with the marinade on the plate first, then place the orange slices and olives on top. Pour over the orange juice and garnish with fennel seeds and fennel leaves.

Lobster

Preparation time: 40 minutes
Cooling time for
  the lobster: 1 hour
Cooking time: 15 minutes
Difficulty: ★

Serves 4

2	lobsters, each 1¼ lb/550 g
1	onion
2 oz/50 g	celery
1	bay leaf
¾ oz/20 g	parsley
½	unwaxed lemon

6 cloves	garlic
¾ oz/20 g	fresh basil
2 tsp/10 g	dried oregano
2 tsp/10 g	dried marjoram
8 oz/200 g	tomatoes
2 oz/50 g	red bell pepper
2 oz/50 g	yellow bell pepper
3 tbsp	olive oil
	salt
	pepper

For the garnish:
  chives

This exquisite salad makes you long to be in Italy. It is easy to prepare and is especially suitable as a cold appetizer for large celebration meals.

The natives of the Adriatic coast are particularly partial to lobster, whose firm, lean, tasty flesh is held in high regard by gourmets everywhere. Lobster is generally steamed or cooked briefly in boiling water, which changes its color from blue-black to brilliant red. Fishmongers always sell lobsters alive. When you buy them, the shells should be intact and the lobsters smell pleasant. The bodies of the males are somewhat elongated, while the females are more compact.

The strong claws, which are dangerous weapons, contain a lot of flesh. The body is divided into seven rings enclosing the soft, delicate meat, and ends in a segmented tail fin. When you cut up the lobster, remove the greenish-colored liver and any coral – the chef uses these to enhance the flavor of the sauce. If you wish, you can substitute crayfish for the lobster.

This lobster salad combines all the flavors of the Mediterranean. Oregano (wild marjoram) has a distinct, mild taste. With its evergreen leaves it is an indispensable ingredient in Italian cookery and goes especially well with tomato dishes. Basil tastes slightly of lemon and jasmine. Although originally from India, the name is from the Greek *basilikos*, meaning "royal." Its leaves are easy to preserve in olive oil. Tomato, the quintessential summer fruit, goes wonderfully well with the red and yellow bell peppers, enhancing the freshness and color of this salad.

Cover the lobsters with boiling water in a saucepan. Add the peeled onion, celery, bay leaf, parsley, and lemon peel. Cover and cook for 6 minutes. Remove the pan from the heat and leave to stand for 2 minutes. Remove the lobsters and leave to cool for 1 hour.

Peel the garlic and blanch in boiling water. Chop the garlic and basil finely and mix with the oregano and marjoram.

Blanch the tomatoes and remove the skins. Cut the bell peppers into quarters, scoop out the seeds, and remove the skin with a vegetable peeler. Cut the bell peppers and tomatoes into small cubes.

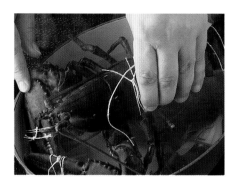

Salad

Remove the legs from the lobster. Cut the claws away from the head, and divide each claw in two. Break open the claws and remove the meat. Reserve the livers, any coral, and the meat from the body.

Put the tomatoes and bell peppers in a dish. Add the seasoning of garlic and herbs and stir. Add the lobster meat and stir again. Fill the shell with the mixture.

To make the sauce, blend 2 ice cubes, the lemon juice, livers, any coral, the olive oil, salt, and pepper. Serve the lobster with the sauce, garnished with chives.

Chicken Salad

Preparation time:	20 minutes
Soaking time:	1 hour
Cooking time:	30 minutes
Difficulty:	☆

Serves 4

4	dried porcini mushrooms (heads)
½	onion
1	carrot
1	stick celery
8 oz/200 g	chicken breast

2 tsp	balsamic vinegar
4 tsp/20 g	pine nuts
1 scant cup/ 225 ml	extra-virgin olive oil
	salt
	pepper

For the garnish:

	basil (to taste)

The Garfagnana mountains, around 20 miles/30 kilometers from Lucca, our chef's native city, are revered by Tuscan gourmets, for it is there they can enjoy the tastiest porcini mushrooms, delicious chestnuts, pecorino cheese, and wonderful spelt dishes.

As early as June and July, but especially in late summer, many people go for walks in the forest in search of porcini mushrooms. The most popular is the *Boletus edulis*, or Bordeaux cep, which tastes good in salads, broiled, in fricassees, in omelets, in soup, or in a delicate pasta sauce.

Since it is virtually impossible to find porcini mushrooms out of season, dried ones are often used. Before soaking them, always wash the dried mushrooms carefully under running water.

Even the simplest Tuscan salad is not complete without a good olive oil to enhance its flavor. Sauro Brunicardi prefers extra-virgin olive oil from Lucca. This has a pronounced green color and is rather cloudy, as it is not filtered. It has a very light, fresh taste, reminiscent of a tart, green apple. In this chicken salad it combines wonderfully well with the subtly flavored balsamic vinegar that comes from Modena.

The pine nuts give the salad some bite and a slightly resinous aroma. The umbrella pine, of which they are the seeds, is part of the Tuscan landscape. Before you use them, make sure they are fresh. Because of their high fat content, they go rancid very quickly. Scatter the roasted pine nuts over the salad after you have garnished it with basil leaves.

Soak the dried porcini mushrooms for 1 hour in lukewarm water, then rinse well. Peel the onion and chop finely. Peel and slice the carrot. Wash the celery and cut into thin slices.

Immerse the onion, carrot, and celery in boiling water and simmer for 10 minutes.

Add the chicken breast to the vegetables. Bring to the boil over a high heat and cook for another 15 minutes.

with Porcini Mushrooms

Cook the mushrooms for 3 minutes in salted water to which 2 drops of balsamic vinegar have been added.

Drain the chicken breast and cut into slices with a sharp knife.

Fry the pine nuts in a skillet without any fat. Arrange a slice of meat and a piece of mushroom alternately on a plate and pour olive oil and a few drops of balsamic vinegar over the top. Season with salt and pepper and garnish with pine nuts and basil.

Sformatini

Preparation time:	1 hour
Soaking time:	overnight
Cooking time for sauce:	20 minutes
Cooking time for sformatino:	1 hour 50 minutes
Difficulty:	★★

Serves 4

For the bean soufflé (sformatino):

12 oz/300 g	white beans
4 tbsp	olive oil
1 stick	celery
1	carrot
1	small onion
1 sprig	fresh rosemary
1⅛ stick/130 g	butter
1 scant cup/100 g	flour

1 cup/250 ml	milk
1 cup/250 ml	cream
2 oz/50 g	parmesan
3	eggs
	salt to taste

For the squid sauce:

4 oz/100 g	small squid
1 clove	garlic
6 sprigs	parsley
1	dried chile
4 tbsp	extra-virgin olive oil
2 tbsp	white wine
⅞ stick/100 g	butter
1 scant cup/100 g	flour
2 cups/500 ml	fish stock
	salt, pepper

The traditional dishes found in the coastal regions of Tuscany include wonderful bean salads with squid. Sauro Brunicardi has drawn inspiration from this original combination to devise these bean soufflés with squid sauce.

The bean soufflés, *sformatini* in Italian, which our chef recommends here are prepared from vegetables and a béchamel sauce made with eggs. They were served as a special delicacy back in the 17th century at Baroque banquets, but they became ordinary family fare in the 19th century.

Spinach, potatoes, artichokes, fennel, zucchini, or cauliflower can be added to the list of ingredients, according to taste. Sauro Brunicardi bakes these soufflés in the oven in little soufflé dishes, but they can also be cooked in a bain marie or in other kinds of dish.

Dried white beans, such as cannellini or white kidney beans, form the basis of the bean soufflé. Beans are widely used in Italian cookery, but cannellini and borlotti beans are extremely popular in Tuscany in particular – to the extent that their compatriots jokingly refer to the Tuscans as *mangiafagioli*, or bean eaters! Although the beans are tender after they have been cooked, their fine shells are still firm; if you purée them, no trace remains of the shells.

The bean soufflés are much improved by the addition of the tasty, white squid sauce. The Italians are familiar with other species related to squid, such as *seppie* (cuttlefish) and their smaller relatives *polipetti* and *moscardini*. The very young squid chosen for this recipe by Sauro Brunicardi are characterized by their soft and delicate flesh and are particularly good in sauces. Shrimp or fish can be substituted for the squid, if preferred.

Sformatini: Soak the beans overnight. Drain and simmer for an hour in salted water. Pour the olive oil into a pan and add the cubed celery, peeled and diced carrot, chopped onion, rosemary, and cooked and drained beans and cook for 10 minutes. Stir.

Prepare a fairly thick béchamel sauce using the butter, flour, and milk. Take the pan with the bean mixture and add the béchamel sauce over high heat. Purée the contents of the pan using a hand blender.

Remove the pan from the heat. Add the cream, grated parmesan, eggs and salt, then stir well. Pour the batter into small, oiled soufflé dishes and bake at 350° F/ 180° C for 30 minutes.

in Squid Sauce

Squid sauce: Prepare and rinse the squid and cut into small pieces. Chop the garlic, parsley, and chile finely and sauté for 3–4 minutes in olive oil. Add the squid and white wine and reduce for 5 minutes over high heat.

In another pan, beat the melted butter with the flour to form a roux. Add the fish stock, season with salt and pepper, and keep stirring until the sauce thickens.

Add the sauce to the sautéed squid. Remove the sformatini from the dishes and arrange each in the center of a plate. Pour over the squid sauce and serve hot.

Deep-fried

Preparation time: 45 minutes
Soaking time: 15 minutes
Cooking time: 1 hour 10 minutes
Difficulty: ★

Serves 4

1	carrot
1 stick	celery
1	onion
1 clove	garlic
2 tbsp	olive oil
1 small piece	butter
4 tbsp	white wine
1 oz/25 g	dried porcini mushrooms

1½ lb/600 g	tomatoes
	salt
12 oz/300 g	Arborio rice
	nutmeg
6 oz/150 g	grated parmesan
2	eggs
2	mozzarella cheeses
12 oz/300 g	breadcrumbs
½ cup/60 g	flour
	oil for deep frying

For the garnish (if desired):
lamb's lettuce

Although the Italians love cooking at home and are very good at it, they often go to eat in one of the many trattorias. Some of the dishes that were once bought and eaten in haste on the street have since entered the realms of gourmet cookery. Typical of the dishes sold by street vendors are *suppli al telefono*, delicious croquettes made from rice, mozzarella, and parmesan that are popular with young and old alike. This dish acquired its name because, when you are eating one, the strands of molten cheese stretch like a telephone cable – rather more appropriate to the days before everyone acquired cordless phones.

Croquettes are normally a symbol of hospitality. Everyone helps prepare them – even the guests. One person begins by forming about a dozen croquettes and passes them on to the next person. It is essential to use a very good extra-virgin olive oil for deep-frying the rice croquettes, and to eat them very hot.

The filling for the croquettes varies according to the region. In northern Italy saffron is popular, sometimes also peas. In Lazio, chicken livers are added. Our chefs wanted to add a personal note, and have suggested enhancing the flavor with porcini mushrooms.

The key ingredient of the dish is mozzarella. It is also called *pasta filata* and is very popular because of its mild, slightly acidic taste. It is produced in Lazio and Campagna and is usually sold in spherical form. Parmesan is the king of Italian cheeses and has a protected designation of origin.

The next time you have guests, why not prepare these delicious *suppli al telefono*, and get them to help you …

Chop the carrot, celery, and onion and fry with the crushed garlic in butter and olive oil. Pour in the white wine after 15 minutes. Soak the dried porcini mushrooms for 15 minutes in lukewarm water and cut into small pieces.

When the white wine has reduced, add the finely diced tomatoes and the mushrooms and season with salt. Simmer for 40 minutes, adding a little more water if necessary.

Boil the rice for about 8 minutes in salted water. Drain and transfer to a dish. Spoon the vegetables on top and stir everything together thoroughly.

Rice Croquettes

Add the nutmeg and parmesan. Then add the eggs and stir thoroughly.

Cut the mozzarella into cubes. Take a small handful of breadcrumbs and then roll some of the rice and vegetable mixture into a ball. Press a piece of mozzarella into the center of each one before sealing the croquette so that the top is domed.

Coat the croquettes firstly in flour, then in breadcrumbs. Deep fry in hot oil until they are golden yellow. Remove and drain. Arrange the croquettes in a circle on a plate and garnish with a few lamb's lettuce leaves in the center.

Soups

Gran Farro

Preparation time:	30 minutes
Soaking time:	overnight
Cooking time:	2 hours 10 minutes
Difficulty:	★★

Serves 4

1¼ lb/500 g	borlotti beans
1	onion
1 stick	celery
1 clove	garlic
4 oz/100 g	slab bacon, with fat
1	carrot
6 oz/150 g	tomatoes

2 tbsp	extra-virgin olive oil
1 sprig	rosemary
4	sage leaves
	marjoram leaves
	salt
	pepper
6 oz/150 g	spelt

For the garnish:

	marjoram
	rosemary
	ground pepper

This recipe is already over a hundred years old. *Gran farro* is a typically Tuscan soup. In this recipe, Sauro Brunicardi shows us one of the recipes mentioned in ancient documents in the Lucca city archives.

Spelt is an easily grown cereal that will flourish even in harsh mountain conditions. Today it is very popular, above all in whole-food recipes. It was one of the staple foods of Etruscan times and later of the poorest people in Rome. One Roman recipe called *puls latina*, for instance, features spelt boiled in water with other kinds of cereal and legumes. With time, "normal" cereals became more widespread, due in part to the fact that the grain and the husk of spelt are firmly attached, so that removal of its husks is very time-consuming.

Tuscan farmers in the mountains of Garfagnana have been cultivating spelt since time immemorial. This hardy cereal thrives on poor ground even without pesticides or chemical fertilizers and is therefore very popular with devotees of organic farming. It is as versatile as ordinary grain and is now available all over Italy.

For this recipe, our chef suggests mixing the spelt with a tasty purée of beans and vegetables. If they are available, use borlotti beans, the small, pinky-beige marbled beans that are classified as red beans (the water in which they are cooked turns reddish in color).

Sauro Brunicardi braises the vegetables lightly in a pan with sage, rosemary, and marjoram. Alternatively, you can braise the vegetables first, then add the herbs at the end.

Soak the beans overnight. Drain and transfer to a saucepan containing cold salted water. Bring to the boil and simmer for at least an hour.

Lift the beans out of the water with a spatula and pass through a strainer to obtain a purée-like consistency. Filter the cooking liquid and set both beans and liquid aside.

Peel the onion and chop finely. Cut the celery into small pieces. Peel the garlic and dice the bacon. Peel and slice the carrot. Blanch the tomatoes, remove the skins, and chop into small pieces.

Lucca Style

Pour the olive oil into a large pan and add the carrot, garlic, celery, onion, tomatoes, bacon cubes, rosemary, sage, and marjoram. Cook for 20 minutes, then pass through a strainer to purée.

Mix the beans with some of the cooking liquid in a pan. Stir in the puréed vegetables, then season with salt and pepper. Bring to the boil.

Rinse the spelt briefly under running water and add to the pan. Simmer over a low heat for 35 to 40 minutes. Pour the gran farro into soup plates and garnish with marjoram, rosemary, and ground pepper. Serve with a dash of extra-virgin olive oil.

Bean

Preparation time: 20 minutes
Soaking time: overnight
Cooking time: 1 hour 55 minutes
Difficulty: ★

Serves 4

1¼ lb/500 g	dried brown beans
4 oz/100 g	celery
1	onion
2 cloves	garlic

1	carrot
2	potatoes
9 tbsp	extra-virgin olive oil
1	tomato
	salt and pepper to taste
1 sprig	rosemary
4–5 oz/120 g	fresh *pappardelle* pasta
	parmesan

Food lovers in the Veneto region have long known the delicious combination pasta and beans can make. Biancarosa Zecchin, who works in Arquà Petrarca, not far from Padua, introduces a soup here made from dried beans, flavorsome vegetables, potatoes, and fresh *pappardelle*, a kind of noodle that comes in broad strips. The dish, which is called *minestra di fagioli* in Italian, is one of the basics in the cuisine of the Veneto, not least because its ingredients are inexpensive.

Great use is made of beans in recipes from the Veneto region. Quite diverse varieties of bean are cultivated in the area between Lamon, Feltre, and Belluno. Beans were once regarded as poor people's fare, but now they also appear on the menu in famous restaurants.

Soak the beans overnight and drain them well before cooking. Even dried beans should not be kept for more than a year; when you open the pack, check to make sure they are not moldy and that there are no tiny holes in the beans – if so, it means they have been attacked by worms!

Rice, small macaroni, or fresh pasta can also be added to this bean soup, as desired. In order to prepare fresh pappardelle, mix two eggs with four glasses of flour and a little salt (serves four). Knead the mixture into a dough and roll it out. Then roll up the dough and cut it into broad slices. Unroll these again and cook them in the soup.

To add a final, flavor-enhancing touch to the soup, sprinkle with some grated parmesan: preferably *parmigiano reggiano*, which is produced in Emilia-Romagna from cow's milk.

Soak the beans overnight. Wash and cut up the celery. Peel the onion, garlic, carrot, and potatoes. Wash, dry, and cut the vegetables into large pieces.

Pour 7 tbsp olive oil into a pan and sauté the garlic briefly before adding the celery, onion, potatoes, and carrots. Simmer for 15 minutes.

Fill the pan with water and add the quartered tomato, salt, pepper, and drained beans. Bring to the boil, cover, and simmer for 30 minutes.

Soup

Remove the vegetables from the broth and pass through a sieve into a saucepan. Thin the resulting purée with the broth and bring to the boil.

Heat the remaining olive oil in a skillet with the chopped rosemary, add to the soup, and bring to the boil again.

Add the pappardelle and stir constantly until the pasta is cooked "al dente." Serve the soup hot. Either sprinkle the grated parmesan on top or serve it separately.

Fisherman's

Preparation time:	20 minutes
Cooking time:	40 minutes
Difficulty:	☆

Serves 4

1½ lb/700 g	small langoustines
12 oz/300 g	small squid
1 lb/400 g	Venus clams
3	tomatoes

1 clove	garlic
4 tbsp	olive oil
	salt
8 oz/200 g	linguini (pasta)

For the garnish:

	parsley

This fisherman's soup is ideal in winter, as it combines all the delicious flavors of the Mediterranean. The dish has a long tradition on the Adriatic coast and is simple to prepare. If you enjoy mussels and crustaceans, this soup could become one of your favorite dishes.

Venus clams, *vongole* in Italian, play a major role in Italian cuisine; *spaghetti alle vongole*, for instance, is very popular all over the country. It is actually possible to eat Venus clams raw, with a little lemon juice. They are easy to recognize from their small yellow to dark gray shells, convex in the middle.

Connoisseurs love langoustines, the taste of which is reminiscent of lobster. It is also a very healthy food, containing a lot of calcium, phosphorus, and iron, and can be prepared in various ways. It is important to remember, however, that crustaceans should only be cooked very briefly. To supplement the range of seafood, Maddalena Beccaceci has also added small squid, which are extremely tender. The tentacles and body sacs are edible, but the ink sac should be removed when cleaning the squid.

The fish stock in which the *linguini* (long noodles, like very fine spaghetti) are cooked and which forms the basis for the soup plays a major part in its success. If you wish to give the soup a stronger flavor, you can add the head of a herring when preparing the stock.

The absence in this recipe of pepper or other strong seasoning allows the flavor of the individual ingredients to develop. Even the garlic is used only to enhance the olive oil and is removed after frying.

Pull the heads off the langoustines and shell the meat. Reserve the heads for the stock. Remove the head and tentacles from the squid, as well as the innards. Skin the squid and remove any hard or rough areas. Wash and slice into small pieces.

For the stock, bring 8 cups/2 l water to the boil in a saucepan and add the langoustine heads. Cover and cook for about 30 minutes.

Put the Venus clams in a saucepan and cover with water. Cook for a few minutes until the clams have opened. Remove the meat. Blanch, skin, and dice the 3 tomatoes.

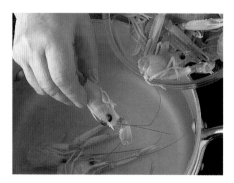

Soup

Fry the whole, peeled garlic clove in olive oil, then remove from the pan. Add the langoustines and fry for about 2 minutes. Then add the squid, Venus clams, and diced tomato. Season with salt and simmer for 5–10 minutes.

Strain the fish stock and bring to the boil. Break the linguini into the pan and cook in the fish stock until the pasta has become "al dente."

Add the seafood and infuse for 1 minute. Pour the soup into bowls and serve sprinkled with chopped parsley.

Spring

Preparation time: 35 minutes
Cooking time: 25 minutes
Difficulty: ★

Serves 4

3½ lb/1.5 kg   small zucchini
1   onion
2 tbsp   olive oil
¾ stick/80 g   butter
                salt
                pepper

4 slices   white, crusty bread
2 cloves   garlic
3   eggs
½ bunch   parsley
                parmesan

For the garnish:
                4 egg yolks (optional)
                mint leaves

Spring Soup is traditional farmer's fare and to a certain extent is symbolic of spring. It is very popular in Lazio, and also in Campagna and Calabria. Easy to prepare, this soup can be eaten hot or cold with bread.

Italian cuisine would be much the poorer without zucchini, which can be cooked in so many different ways – braised, broiled, fried, stuffed, or in salads – and are an essential ingredient in this soup. With their high water content and low nutritional value, zucchini grow in abundance in the southern part of the Italian peninsula. When buying, choose small ones, as these are especially tender. Make sure that they are firm at the ends and unblemished. Zucchini can be eaten either peeled or unpeeled, but in any event should be washed thoroughly. Depending on the season, you can substitute white beet or pumpkin.

This soup, which is highly nutritious thanks to the eggs, cheese, butter, and bread, is greatly enhanced by the addition of parsley. This aromatic plant, which is available all year round, is an essential ingredient in Italian cuisine. It should be fresh and crisp, with firm stalks and leaves.

Garlic is also available throughout the year. It tastes milder in spring and is easier to peel. In cultivation for over 5,000 years, garlic belongs to the labiate genus of plants and is said to be very good for the circulation. Only use firm, fat cloves.

In southern Italy, pecorino, an air-dried ewe's milk cheese, is normally used to enhance the flavor of this soup. In this recipe, however, Marco and Rosella Folicaldi prefer to use parmesan.

Wash and dice the zucchini.

Peel the onion and chop coarsely. Sauté in olive oil and butter, then add the diced zucchini. Cover and simmer for 10–20 minutes, adding water if necessary. Season with salt and pepper.

Toast the crusty bread. Rub with the peeled garlic cloves and set aside.

Soup

Beat the eggs in a small bowl. Add the chopped parsley and beat again.

Add the beaten eggs to the zucchini and stir with a wooden spoon.

Grate parmesan over the soup. Season to taste with pepper. Serve the soup in bowls with the bread. If desired, add an egg yolk to each serving and garnish with mint leaves.

Vegetable

Preparation time:	*30 minutes*		1	marrow bone
Cooking time:	*3 hours 25 minutes*		4 oz/100 g	carrots
Difficulty:	★		4 oz/100 g	celery
			4 oz/100 g	onions

Serves 4

8 oz/200 g	zucchini
8 oz/200 g	celery
4 oz/100 g	carrots
4 oz/100 g	*orecchiette* (pasta)
	salt
	pepper

1	marrow bone
4 oz/100 g	carrots
4 oz/100 g	celery
4 oz/100 g	onions
1 pinch	thyme
2	bay leaves
2 cloves	garlic

For the garnish:

olive oil
toasted bread

For the stock:

8 oz/200 g	topside of beef
8 oz/200 g	beef shoulder

In Italy, vegetable soup – which is usually made with pasta or rice – is called *minestrone*. This soup, which is almost a vegetarian dish, has many regional variations. White beans, zucchini, onions, leeks, tomatoes, carrots, and cabbage are essential ingredients in Tuscany, while the Genoese often prefer to use pumpkin, broad beans, red kidney beans, celery, and tomatoes.

The vitamin-laden soup devised by Sergio Pais is easy to prepare and, thanks to the *orecchiette*, is highly nourishing. This pasta, shaped like small ears, is particularly popular in southern Italy. In its native Bari it is also known as *paciocchi*.

Sergio Pais ensures that the soup is robust and full of flavor by first preparing a stock made from beef, marrowbone, carrots, celery, onions, and herbs, in which the vegetables are then cooked.

Zucchini are absolutely indispensable in Mediterranean cookery and are available from markets everywhere during the summer. They are cultivated mainly in southern Italy, where they are harvested 4–6 days after flowering. Originally from Central America, they were used only for decorative purposes when first introduced to Europe, but they are now used in many dishes. Buy small, evenly colored zucchini and peel them finely before cutting them into small pieces.

The celery gives the vegetable soup its characteristic aroma and fresh taste. The area around Trevi has been well known for cultivating celery since the 17th century.

Enjoy this fresh, healthy, aromatic soup!

For the stock, heat 8 cups/2 l water in a large saucepan. Add the beef and marrowbone. Simmer for 2–2½ hours, removing the froth occasionally.

After three-quarters of the cooking time, add the peeled carrots, celery, onions, thyme, bay leaves, and garlic.

Wash and wipe the zucchini, celery, and carrots and cut into small cubes.

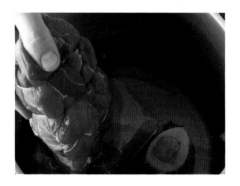

Soup

Remove the meat, bones, and vegetables from the saucepan and strain the stock.

Add the diced vegetables to the stock and simmer for 25 minutes.

After a good 15 minutes, add the orecchiette to the simmering vegetables and season with salt and pepper. Pour the soup into bowls and serve with a dash of olive oil and slices of toasted bread.

Barley Soup

Preparation time: 50 minutes
Cooking time: 55 minutes
Difficulty: ☆

Serves 4

1	zucchini
1	carrot
1	leek
1	radicchio
3 tbsp	vegetable oil
½ stick/60 g	butter
2	bay leaves
	salt
	pepper

1½ cups/300 g	pearl barley

4 cups/1 l	milk
2 slices	bacon

For the croquettes:

12 oz/300 g	grated *Cantal* cheese, mild
3½ tbsp/50 g	grated parmesan
4 tsp/20 g	flour
2	eggs
4 oz/100 g	breadcrumbs
2 cups/500 ml	oil for deep frying

For the garnish:

	parsley

The high plain of Asagio in South Tyrol has been famous for its milk for over a thousand years. According to Francesca de Giovannini, the Germanic Cimbri tribe brought their herds to graze the pastures and settled there, subsisting mainly on barley and milk.

Our chef is very interested in the history of her region and has therefore provided us with an ancient recipe that is said to date back to the time of the Cimbri. During the course of the centuries, the soup has been enriched with seasonal vegetables. This recipe is also enhanced by the addition of cheese croquettes and slices of bacon, typical specialties of the region.

Barley, a very hardy cereal, is cultivated in Italy mainly in South Tyrol and Friuli. The husks are removed from the long, pointed grains, which are then ground between two millstones into small, round pearls. Pearl barley is especially suitable for soups, but spelt can be used instead.

Francesca de Giovannini's peasant-style soup is almost a vegetable soup. In South Tyrol, the radicchio, a red endive from Treviso, is very popular; connoisseurs even hold events in its honor. This crunchy vegetable can be eaten raw or cooked, broiled or stuffed. It is easily recognized by its violet color and white ribs and is available on all the market stalls from December onward. Zucchini, with their high water content, are also an indispensable ingredient in Mediterranean cuisine, and are grown mainly in southern Italy. When buying, choose those of uniform color.

This nutritious, Cimbri-style barley soup is an ideal dish for the winter months.

Wash and wipe the zucchini, carrot, leek, and radicchio, and then dice very finely.

Heat 2 tbsp vegetable oil and ⅜ stick/50 g butter in a large saucepan. Add the diced vegetables and bay leaves. Season with salt and pepper and sauté for 3 minutes. Mix in the barley.

Pour in the milk and stir. Simmer over medium heat for 40–50 minutes.

Cimbri Style

For the croquettes, mix the Cantal cheese, parmesan, flour, and 1 whole egg in a salad bowl and knead to a smooth dough. Beat the remaining egg in a small bowl.

Roll the dough into a thin roll and cut into pieces about the width of a finger. Roll each piece into a ball in the palms of your hands. Dip in the egg and then breadcrumbs. Deep-fry in oil.

Heat the remaining vegetable oil and butter in a pan and brown the bacon. Serve the soup with the croquettes and bacon, with chopped parsley scattered on top.

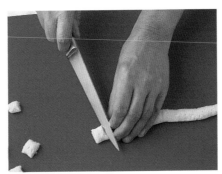

Pumpkin

Preparation time:	45 minutes
Cooking time:	50 minutes
Difficulty:	★★

Serves 4

1	pumpkin weighing about 3¼ lb/1.5 kg
5	medium-sized potatoes
6	onions
3 cloves	garlic
1	dried chile
5	sage leaves
1 sprig	rosemary
4 tbsp	olive oil
2 tbsp	flour

| 4 tbsp | red wine |
| 3 (400 g) cans | tomatoes |

| | salt |
| | pepper |

For the polenta:

1½ cups/250 g	semolina
1 tsp	salt
	nutmeg

To serve:

| 5 tbsp | grated pecorino cheese |

For the garnish:

| | sage leaves |
| 1 sprig | rosemary |

This pumpkin ragout with polenta is an extremely unusual dish, although vegetable ragouts are typical of southern Italy. The inventive inhabitants used to draw a veil over the absence of meat in their everyday fare by humorously re-naming various vegetable dishes with evocative names such as "Doves from Paradise" or "Soup made from anchovies still in the sea." Our pumpkin ragout is just such a dish.

For this dish, which is easy to prepare, Marco and Rossella Folicaldi suggest that the ragout is served in the pumpkin, which is brought to the table whole. They have developed a real passion for pumpkins, so it comes as no surprise to learn that their restaurant in Nice is called "La zucca magica," i.e., the magic pumpkin.

Shortly after being introduced to Italy by the Spaniards, who had brought the pumpkin from the New World, it soon acquired the name *zucca*, which originally meant "nincompoop" in the vernacular.

The warm, orange-red color of the pumpkins glows in market stall displays. This winter vegetable is especially popular in Venice, where street vendors sell slices of roasted pumpkin; it is rich in vitamin A and has a subtle flavor all of its own.

Sage and rosemary give this ragout its unusual aroma. Marco and Rossella Folicaldi recommend serving it with a polenta dish made from semolina. For a more substantial polenta, use milk instead of water. Add a dash of olive oil before serving.

Using a large knife, cut off a large section of the stalk end of the pumpkin, like a lid. Scoop out the flesh with a spoon and set it aside.

Peel the potatoes and dice coarsely. Cut the pumpkin flesh into small pieces. Peel the onions and cloves of garlic and chop finely.

Sauté the onions, garlic, finely chopped chile, sage leaves, and sprig of rosemary in olive oil in a large saucepan. Add the pumpkin flesh and the potatoes. Sprinkle flour over the top to thicken.

with Polenta

Pour in the wine and reduce. Add the tomatoes and season with salt and pepper. Simmer for about 40 minutes.

For the polenta, heat 2 cups/500 ml water and pour in the semolina. Stir with a balloon whisk. Season with salt and nutmeg. Cook for 3 minutes.

Transfer the polenta to small dishes. Fill the hollowed-out pumpkin with the mixture from the saucepan and bring the pumpkin to the table. Garnish with sage and rosemary, and serve with grated pecorino cheese.

Zuppa

Preparation time: 40 minutes
Cooking time: 35 minutes
Difficulty: ★

Serves 4

1¼ lb/500 g	Venus clams
5 cloves	garlic
5 tbsp	olive oil
¼ bunch	parsley
8 oz/200 g	sausagemeat

	salt
	pepper
2 sprigs	rosemary
4 tbsp	white wine
12 oz/300 g	potatoes

For the garnish:

parsley

Alberto Melagrana thinks that the Marche region must be very like Paradise. He is so much in love with this region that his praise for the variety and quality of the produce here, which the natives of the area are fortunate enough to have in abundance, knows no bounds. The richly endowed region is the source of many sophisticated and original recipes like this one.

Zuppa Picena is a typical soup from the province of Picena and was traditionally prepared on fishing boats. Before they set sail, the seamen took their provisions on board, storing potatoes in the hold and hanging sausages from the mast. Depending on what they caught in their nets, they would prepare a soup that would remind them of dishes they ate at home. Today, *zuppa Picena* is eaten mainly in winter, sometimes with the addition of toasted slices of white bread.

Venus clams are easily recognizable from their small, convex shells. They are highly prized in Italy for their tasty flesh and go wonderfully well with white wine, tomatoes, shallots, and thyme. If they are unavailable, it is possible to substitute Tellini mussels, which should be cleaned the night before.

Farmers in the Marche region used to slaughter their pigs themselves. Surplus meat was distributed among their neighbors or made into sausages. These sausages, which kept for a long time, were also popular with fishermen on the coast. Italian sausage is typically made from coarsely chopped meat and is not highly seasoned. The meat is often used in sauces and ragouts.

Clean the Venus clams under running water. Sauté 4 cloves garlic in 4 tbsp olive oil and add the clams. Cover and simmer briefly until the clams have opened. Scatter the chopped parsley over the top.

Form the sausagemeat into even-sized small balls and brown them in a pan with the remaining olive oil. Season with salt and pepper. Add the remaining garlic and a sprig of rosemary. Sauté for 3–4 minutes before pouring in the white wine.

Peel the potatoes and cut into small even-sized cubes.

Picena

Place the potatoes in a pan of boiling water and cook with the other sprig of rosemary. Drain.

Carefully transfer the Venus clams, potatoes, and meatballs to a saucepan.

Pour over 2 cups/500 ml boiling water and simmer for 5 minutes. Pour the soup into bowls and garnish with parsley.

Pasta &
Rice

Bigoli with

Preparation time:	20 minutes
Cooking time:	35 minutes
Difficulty:	★★

Serves 4

½	duck
1 clove	garlic
1	onion
1 tbsp	olive oil

2 sprigs	rosemary
7 tbsp	dry white wine
	salt
	pepper
1½ lb/700 g	bigoli (pasta)

To serve:

grated parmesan

For the garnish:

bay leaves
rosemary

Biancarosa Zecchin's recipe, which is a traditional dish from the Veneto region presented here in its original form, features fresh pasta in a piquant sauce of duck meat, onion, garlic, and rosemary, cooked in white wine.

Bigoli is a type of pasta that resembles spaghetti, but is rather thicker and rolled up into "nests." As these are egg noodles, they are not often available in stores, but are usually prepared at home. To serve four people, take 1½ pounds/700 grams flour, 2 eggs, and a scant ½ cup/100 milliliters water and mix together. Form the resulting dough into a ball and then roll out. If you do not have a pasta machine, cut the dough with a knife into long, very thin strips. If you prefer wider strips, you can buy *pappardelle*.

The natives of the Veneto region traditionally use a *torchio* or *bigolaro*, a hand-operated press on a tripod, to make pasta. The dough is fed into a tube 4 inches/10 centimeters in diameter, at the end of which various different attachments can be fitted. If you insert the attachment for *bigoli* and turn the handle, the corresponding shape of pasta will be produced and will fall onto a grid to dry. Only a few families were fortunate enough to own a *bigolaro*, so if you wanted to make noodles it was a good time to meet up with friends or relatives.

If the duck has too much fat on it, remove the thick layer under the skin before you start cooking. Then cut the flesh into small cubes. During cooking, the combination of duck and rosemary produces a wonderful flavor.

Skin the duck and remove the fat if necessary. Place the duck, breast side up, on a board and cut in half lengthways, separating the meat from the bones. Cut into even-sized ¼ in/5 mm cubes.

Peel the garlic and onion and chop into small pieces. Heat the olive oil in a large pan and add the garlic and onion. Sauté for 2–3 minutes and scatter the chopped rosemary on top. Leave to infuse for a short while.

Add the cubed duck meat to the mixture. Cook for 10–15 minutes and stir well until all the liquid has been absorbed.

Duck Ragout

Pour in the white wine and season with salt and pepper. Cook for a further 5 minutes, stirring constantly.

Boil the bigoli in plenty of salted water until they are cooked "al dente," then drain.

Mix the bigoli with the duck sauce. Sprinkle the grated parmesan over the top, garnish with bay leaves and rosemary, and serve hot.

Potato Gnocchi

Preparation time: 30 minutes
Cooking time: 1 hour
Difficulty: ★★

Serves 4

For the gnocchi:
2¼ lb/1 kg   potatoes
             salt
2 cups/225 g flour

For the sauce:
1 stick   celery
1   carrot

1   onion
2 cloves   garlic
1½ lb/700 g   tomatoes
4 tbsp/60 ml   extra-virgin olive oil
               salt
               pepper
20   small thyme leaves

To serve:
8 tsp/40 g   grated pecorino

The restaurant "La Mora" in Ponte a Moriano (the name means "rest" or "pause" in Latin) dates back to 1867. It is a very inviting place to stop after touring the countryside around Lucca. Sauro Brunicardi and his colleague Paolo Indragoli recommend one of its specialties, potato *gnocchi* with a simple, highly piquant vegetable sauce.

Gnocchi – meaning "little dumplings" – have been produced mainly in northern and central Italy since the 18th century, when the parcels of dough were called *ravioli* (ravioli as we know them used to be called *tortellini*). Today, two main types are produced: those made from potatoes and flour, and those made from semolina with spinach and ricotta.

Although *gnocchi* look easy enough to prepare, a certain amount of skill is needed to achieve an acceptable-looking result. The dough must be light, yet firm, and must not disintegrate in the sauce during cooking. Floury potato varieties such as bintje give the right consistency. Knead the mixture as you would pastry dough. Then cut the *gnocchi* on a floured surface, so they do not stick.

The sauce should be thick enough to coat the *gnocchi* well. Italians traditionally serve tomato sauce with basil or pesto with nuts and gorgonzola as an accompaniment to *gnocchi*. Sauro Brunicardi passes the vegetables for the sauce through a sieve to remove the skins and seeds. The resulting, smooth purée goes wonderfully well with thyme and pecorino, a ewe's milk cheese that gives the dish its typically Tuscan character. After maturing for four months, the cheese is the color of straw; it develops its full flavor in this dish.

For the gnocchi, boil the unpeeled potatoes in salted water for 20 minutes. Drain, peel, cut into large pieces, and pass through a sieve. Leave to cool slowly.

Sprinkle some flour over the work surface. Knead the lukewarm potato with about 1¾ cups/200 g flour, until it no longer sticks to your fingers.

Divide the potato dough into portions, rolling each one into a long tube a finger's breadth in diameter. Cut into pieces about ¾ in/2 cm in length.

"Mora"

For the sauce, clean the celery and carrot, then slice. Peel the onion and garlic and chop finely. Quarter the tomatoes. Put the oil in a pan, add the vegetables, season with salt and pepper, and cook over high heat for 25–30 minutes.

In a large saucepan, bring some salted water to the boil and add a few drops of oil. Cook the gnocchi in the boiling water until they rise to the surface.

Strain the cooked vegetables through a sieve and transfer to a large pan with the gnocchi and a few thyme leaves. Stir well and bring to the boil. Serve with grated pecorino.

Lasagne

Preparation time: 50 minutes
Cooking time: 1 hour
Difficulty: ☆

Serves 4

2	eggplants
2	zucchini
2	large onions
2	very young artichokes
1	lemon
4 tbsp	white wine
4 tbsp	balsamic vinegar
4 tbsp	olive oil
	salt
	pepper

10 oz/250 g	lasagne
10 tbsp/150 g	grated parmesan

For the béchamel sauce:

scant ½ stick/ 50 g	butter
scant ½ cup/ 50 g	flour
2 cups/500 ml	milk
	salt
	pepper
1 pinch	grated nutmeg

For the garnish:

	arugula

Sergio Pais named his restaurant in Paris "La Rucola" – "arugula" – as a result of his love for this Mediterranean salad plant. This recipe, a vegetable lasagne, is one of the specialties on the menu.

The natives of Bologna regard themselves as the unassailable champions when it comes to preparing lasagne. Normally these long, rectangular sheets of pasta, originally from Emilia-Romagna, are layered alternately with minced meat and béchamel sauce. Here is a tip, should you need to serve your lasagne in smaller portions: Leave the prepared dish to cool for about three hours, then you can easily cut it to individual requirements.

This northern Italian specialty is inconceivable without béchamel sauce, which is made from a roux of flour and milk. It was traditionally made with cream, which produced a wonderfully thick, velvety sauce.

When you have cleaned the small, violet artichokes, immerse them in water containing lemon juice to stop them discoloring. If you want to keep them for a few days, leave the stalks on.

Zucchini, a classic summer vegetable, adds color.

Eggplants are popular throughout the Mediterranean region. The most common variety is purple-skinned, and is the one used by Sergio Pais in this recipe.

Give this simple recipe a try – it is sure to be popular with family and friends.

Wash the eggplants and zucchini and cut these, together with the peeled onions, into even-sized cubes. Remove the outer leaves from the artichokes until you reach the hearts, then immerse them in water with a dash of lemon juice.

Pour 2 cups/500 ml water into a saucepan with the white wine and balsamic vinegar and boil the artichokes in this liquid for about 20 minutes. Drain. Remove the "choke" and cut the flesh into small pieces.

Braise the onions, eggplants, and zucchini in the olive oil in another pan, and drain on kitchen paper.

"Rucola"

For the béchamel sauce, melt the butter and stir in the flour. Add the milk, stirring constantly. Season with salt and pepper, and sprinkle with nutmeg.

Add the onions, zucchini, eggplants, and artichokes to the béchamel sauce. Stir carefully and adjust seasoning to taste. Reserve a few of the diced vegetables for the garnish.

Layer the lasagne sheets with the sauce in an ovenproof dish and sprinkle with parmesan. Bake for 30 minutes at 350° F/180° C. Place a serving of lasagne on each plate and garnish with a drizzle of oil, the remaining diced vegetables, and arugula.

Paccheri

Preparation time:	20 minutes
Cooking time:	2 hours 10 minutes
Difficulty:	☆

Serves 4

8 oz/200 g	boned breast of lamb
4 leaves	basil
4 tbsp	red wine
	pepper
6 tbsp	olive oil
1	onion
	salt

10 oz/250 g	tomatoes
12 oz/300 g	paccheri di gragniano (pasta)
6 oz/150 g	grated Caciocavallo cheese

For the garnish

4 leaves	basil
	oil for deep frying

According to Michelina Fischetti, the actor Eduardo De Filippo spoke often of a famous Neapolitan goulash he had greatly enjoyed, from a very young age. This substantial goulash is traditionally served at weddings. It is simple to prepare and absolutely delicious. The meat from a breast of lamb is braised slowly with tomatoes, onion, and red wine, to which the main accompaniment is pasta – in the Neapolitan region, this is *paccheri*, which is Neapolitan for "a box on the ears." *Paccheri* are small, thick tubes, and it is therefore possible to substitute macaroni in this recipe.

Many historians believe that the Chinese invented pasta, while others attribute the invention to imperial Rome. The Romans are known to have eaten noodles made from flour and water, which they called *langanum*. The Neapolitans like to think that pasta was invented at the foot of Vesuvius. Although this is not entirely consistent with historical fact, given that pasta has only been eaten there since the end of the 18th century, a wide range of ingenious variations have nevertheless originated in Naples. Originally known as *mangiafoglia*, or "leaf eaters," the Neapolitans have subsequently come to be known as *mangiamaccheroni*, or "pasta eaters."

The fresh flavor of tomato plays an important role in the success of this goulash. Tomatoes are an indispensable part of Mediterranean cuisine and can undoubtedly be described as the favorite vegetable of the Italians. They are grown mainly in southern Italy, which supplies the north of the country with tomatoes and, in addition, exports them all over the world. It took some considerable time for tomatoes to find their way onto the table at the Neapolitan royal palace; serious cultivation probably did not begin until the mid-18th century.

Our chef recommends *caciocavallo*, the southern Italian version of parmesan, to go with the *paccheri*.

Cut the meat into small pieces with a knife. Deep-fry 4 basil leaves for the garnish. Tear the other 4 leaves into small pieces and set aside.

Transfer the lamb into a salad bowl and cover with water. Pour in 2 tbsp red wine, mix, and leave for a few moments to infuse. Drain the meat and season with pepper.

Pour the olive oil into a pan. Peel and chop the onion and sauté until transparent. Add the lamb and brown for 5 minutes. Season with salt.

with Lamb Goulash

Add the remaining red wine and reduce. Wash, blanch, and skin the tomatoes and sieve to make a purée.

Add the tomato purée to the meat. Simmer for 2 hours, then add the torn basil leaves.

Boil the paccheri in salted water until cooked "al dente." Drain. Pour the goulash over the pasta and mix. Transfer the paccheri onto plates, sprinkle with the cheese, and garnish with deep-fried basil leaves.

Pizza

Preparation time: 1 hour
Resting time for
   the dough: 1 hour
Cooking time: 25 minutes
Difficulty: ✳✳

Serves 4

1 lb/400 g	cherry tomatoes
3 tbsp	olive oil
¾ lb/350 g	buffalo mozzarella

For the dough:

5 tsp/25 g	beer yeast
4⅓ cups/	
500 g	flour
	salt

For the garnish:

	basil leaves
	olive oil

To invent pizza, you would probably have had to be born at the foot of Vesuvius. Today there are endless variations on this Neapolitan specialty that is now world-famous. Although the Italians proudly claim that you can use anything you like as a topping – Venus clams, mussels, sausage, ham, arugula, paprika, onions, artichokes, capers, olives, and different types of cheese – purists know that the topping of a *pizza Napoli* consists only of tomatoes, mozzarella, basil, and olive oil. The pizza baker Raffaele Esposito is said to have devised this pizza topping with the colors of the Italian royal kingdom – green, white, and red – in honor of Queen Margherita in 1889.

With the mass exodus from Italy to America, the traditional pizza, as well as many other varieties, reached the New World and achieved hitherto unknown popularity, with the result that the first pizzeria was opened in New York in 1905. *Pizza Napoli* would certainly never have been such a success had it not been for the many years of experience of the Neapolitan pizza bakers, as everything depends on the preparation of the dough. This should be rolled out to about ¼ inch/5 millimeters in depth.

The flavor of the tomatoes used is crucial. During the 19th century, the Neapolitans pioneered various procedures that enabled them to eat tomatoes all year round. Today, we have canned, peeled tomatoes to fall back on.

In Naples, a pizza without mozzarella would be tantamount to heresy. The traditional spherical cheese from Campagna is held in high regard because of its mild, acidic taste.

This southern Italian specialty can be served equally well as a appetizer or a main dish. As the Italians say, it is, quite simply, *buonissima*.

For the dough, stir the yeast into warm water. Put the flour in a bowl and make a hollow in the middle. Pour the yeast mixture into the hollow and add salt.

Using your hands, gradually knead 2 cups/500 ml water into the dough until it is elastic and comes away from the sides of the bowl. Cover with a damp cloth and leave to rise for 1 hour.

Wash the cherry tomatoes and crush between your hands to remove the seeds from them.

Napoli

Roll the ball of dough in flour. Dust the work surface with flour and roll out the dough with a rolling pin until you have a thin, flat circle to fit your baking sheet.

Pour 2 tbsp olive oil over the tomatoes. Grease the baking sheet with the remaining oil. Cover the sheet with the dough and distribute the tomatoes over the top. Bake for about 20 minutes at 450° F/ 230° C.

Remove the pizza from the oven and sprinkle with mozzarella cubes. Bake for a further 5 minutes at 450° F/230° C. Garnish with basil leaves and serve drizzled with olive oil.

Rice Potatoes

Preparation time: 1 hour
Cooking time: 1 hour
Difficulty: ★★

Serves 4

1¾ lb/800 g	large potatoes
4 oz/100 g	shrimp
1 stick	celery
1 scant cup/ 200 ml	white wine
10 tbsp	extra-virgin olive oil

1 clove	garlic
1	fresh chile
6 oz/160 g	mussels
6 oz/160 g	Venus clams
6 oz/160 g	cockles
⅗ cup/120 g	Carnaroli rice (or other risotto rice)

Alfonso Caputo has been inspired by the tasty seafood from the Tyrrhenian Sea to devise a stuffing for potatoes, making a shrimp stock that enhances the rice as well as the sauce.

Fishermen in the Bay of Naples have been hauling in catches of delicious seafood since time immemorial, even though environmental pollution and intensive fishing have recently made this more difficult. Venus clams are rather thick, and easily recognizable by their beige and brown striped shells. Cockles, on the other hand, are smaller and have a thicker shell with deep, concentric ridges. Mussels make the heart of every Neapolitan chef beat faster. Brush them thoroughly under running water, scrape the shells clean with a knife, and remove the beards. You should rinse the mussels again just before cooking.

The stock forms the basis for the seafood sauce and is prepared using the shrimp shells, white wine, and celery. You can also add leek, carrot, onions, or chives, according to personal taste.

Choose a floury variety of potato. Risotto rice is recommended for the filling, since the grains expand without sticking together. If at all possible use Carnaroli rice, which is cultivated on the Po plain, but Vialone-Nano or Arborio rice will do just as well. The rice is cooked in two stages: After simmering for ten minutes in the stock, it is drained and set aside to cool before being cooked in the oven. Alfonso Caputo recommends serving one stuffed potato per person with the delicious sauce.

Wash the potatoes and pat them dry. Cut horizontally across each end. Hollow out the potatoes and blanch for 5 minutes in boiling water.

Shell the shrimp. Sauté the heads and shells in a saucepan with the chopped celery. When they begin to turn red, quench with half the white wine and top up the pan with water. Bring to the boil, cook for 5 minutes, and strain the stock.

Heat 5 tbsp oil in a skillet with ½ clove garlic and the chile. Add the cleaned shellfish, cover, and cook for 5 minutes. Remove the lid and discard any shellfish that are still closed. Remove the meat from the shells and set aside, then strain the sauce and put aside.

with Mussels

Fry the rice with the garlic in the remaining oil. Pour in the rest of the white wine and the strained shrimp stock. Simmer for 10 minutes then strain, reserving the sauce and setting the rice aside to cool.

Boil the shellfish in the sauce for 2–3 minutes over high heat. Add half the shrimp and simmer for a few more minutes. Sauté the remaining shrimp in a skillet for 3–4 minutes.

Fill the potatoes with the rice and fried shrimp. Transfer the potatoes to an ovenproof dish and cook in the oven for 10–15 minutes at 350° F/180° C. Arrange a potato in the center of each plate and serve with the seafood sauce.

Herb Orzotto

Preparation time: 30 minutes
Cooking time: 1 hour 20 minutes
Difficulty: ★★

Serves 4

4	sage leaves
10	mint leaves
12 oz/300 g	spinach
10	basil leaves
2 tsp/10 g	chopped parsley
2 oz/50 g	fennel

12	large shrimp
½	onion
1	carrot
1 stick	celery
3	shallots
2 tbsp	extra-virgin olive oil
1¼ cups/ 250 g	pearl barley
	salt
	pepper
scant ½ stick/ 50 g	butter

This outstanding *orzotto* from Friuli, which is related to risotto, originally from Lombardy, used to be prepared as a soup with pearl barley as the basic ingredient. Paolo Zoppalatti, however, prefers to make it with a less liquid consistency, skillfully seasoning it with a mixture of aromatic herbs and enhancing it with shrimp.

An *orzotto* is cooked in the same way as a risotto: The grains are fried in a pan with the shallots and then quenched with the herb stock that is subsequently reduced. The first step when preparing the dish is to make an original stock from sage, mint, spinach, basil, and fennel. Blanch the herbs and vegetables briefly and transfer to a dish containing ice cubes. This interrupts the cooking process, so that the herbs retain their chlorophyll and hence their beautiful green color. They will be needed again later to give the barley its color and flavor.

In Italy, barley is grown mainly in Friuli and South Tyrol. It dates back thousands of years and flourishes in poor soil and harsh climatic conditions. The grains are of similar diameter and color as grains of wheat, but are rather longer and more pointed. In Friuli, barley is frequently ground and used as flour, but the grains are also used with the husks removed or as pearl barley: in other words, milled until the grains are spherical.

Shrimp play a dual role in this recipe: The heads give flavor to the herb stock and the delicious flesh enhances the *orzotto*. The Friuli and Venezia Giulia regions lie on the northern Adriatic coast, where the fishing industry is still very important. The inhabitants of the lagoons of Grado and Marano continue to catch large quantities of mullet, perch, turbot, and various types of crab. Other crustaceans or mussels can successfully be substituted for the shrimp.

Finely chop the sage, mint, spinach, basil, and parsley. Cut the fennel into large pieces. Blanch all these ingredients in boiling water for 1 minute.

Remove the herbs with a spatula and transfer immediately to a small bowl of ice cubes. Set the herbs and stock aside.

Remove the heads from the shrimp. Peel the tails and dice the flesh, reserving 4 whole tails for the garnish. Set aside.

with Shrimp

Strain the herb stock into a saucepan. Add the onion, carrot, celery stalk and leaves, and shrimp heads. Simmer for about 40 minutes.

Fry the chopped shallots gently in the olive oil for about 5 minutes, until they are soft and transparent. Stir in the pearl barley and sauté for 3 minutes, stirring constantly. Mix in the diced shrimp.

Add a little herb stock to the barley mixture. Cook for 20 minutes. Gradually pour in the remaining stock. Add the blanched herbs. Season with salt and pepper. Leave to infuse for 10 minutes before adding the butter. Serve the orzotto on soup plates, garnished with shrimp tails.

Ravioli

Preparation time: 40 minutes
Resting time for
   the dough: 30 minutes
Cooking time: 15 minutes
Difficulty: ★★★

Serves 4

For the dough:
6½ cups/	
750 g	flour
5	eggs
2 tbsp	olive oil
	salt

For the filling:
6 oz/150 g	spinach
12 oz/300 g	ricotta

2 oz/50 g	grated parmesan
1 pinch	grated nutmeg
1	egg
	salt
	pepper

For the sauce:
3 oz/70 g	pine nuts
9 oz/220 g	basil
2 oz/50 g	marjoram leaves
⅞ stick/	
100 g	butter
1 scant cup/	
200 ml	light cream
	salt

Sauro Brunicardi has an excellent dish of ravioli with marjoram on the menu at his restaurant in Ponte a Moriano. Tuscan ravioli is usually prepared with a stuffing made from pork and beef or veal. In contrast, our chef's light filling is simply made from ricotta, spinach, parmesan, and eggs.

There are around 300 different kinds of pasta in Italy. Fresh stuffed pasta, such as ravioli, seems to have been eaten in Renaissance times; such delicacies apparently arrived in Tuscany, which is regarded today as a true pasta-lover's paradise, from Emilia-Romagna. The ravioli dough is prepared in the classic manner: A hollow is made in the flour, the other ingredients are placed in it, and everything is then kneaded into a dough, working from the center outwards. If the dough becomes too stiff, simply add a little water and continue to knead.

The basic ingredient for the filling of this ravioli is ricotta, made by reheating the whey from fresh ewe's milk cheese. This is why it acquired the name *ricotta*, which literally means "cooked again."

With his ravioli, Sauro Brunicardi serves a cream and herb sauce with the wonderfully fresh, piquant flavors of basil and marjoram. A small, bushy plant, marjoram is a relative of oregano and is one of the classic herbs in Italian cuisine. Its small, pale green leaves, which taste of mint and lemon, have been used to enhance dishes since Ancient Roman times.

Whether round, square, or crescent-shaped, a portion of six or seven ravioli will delight your guests.

For the dough, place the flour in a heap on the work surface and make a hollow in the center. Place the eggs, oil, a pinch of salt, and a scant ½ cup/100 ml water in the hollow and knead all the ingredients together. Leave to stand for 30 minutes.

For the filling, wash the spinach and blanch for 4–5 minutes in boiling, salted water. Drain, then finely chop. Mix with the ricotta.

Add the grated parmesan and nutmeg. Beat in the egg and season with salt and pepper. Knead again thoroughly.

with Marjoram

Roll out the pasta dough thinly on a floured work surface and cut into wide strips. Using two small spoons, place small heaps of filling in the middle of the strips at regular intervals.

Place another strip of pasta dough on top of the strip with the filling and use your fingertips to press the dough around and in between the little domes of filling. Cut out the ravioli with a circular cutter. Cook for 5 minutes in salted water, then drain.

For the sauce, mix together 2 oz/50 g pine nuts, 8 oz/200 g basil, the marjoram, softened butter, cream, and salt, and heat in a pan. Stir in the ravioli, then transfer to plates and garnish with the remaining roasted pine nuts and basil.

Black

Preparation time:	*35 minutes*
Cooking time:	*2 hours 25 minutes*
Difficulty:	★★

Serves 4

12 oz/300 g	cuttlefish
½	onion
⅔ cup/150 ml	olive oil
2 cups/400 g	Arborio rice
4 cups/1 l	fish stock

	salt
	pepper
1 clove	garlic
1	cuttlefish ink sac
4 tbsp/60 g	grated parmesan
⅞ stick/100 g	butter

For the garnish:

	parsley
	cherry tomatoes
	(optional)

This black risotto, which is very popular in Venice, has a long tradition on the Adriatic coast. Today, this delicious cuttlefish dish also has a following in other regions.

Black risotto is very easy to prepare and has a subtle flavor. The cuttlefish are around 12 inches/30 centimeters long, and live on the seabed in coastal waters. They are easily recognized by their gray-beige, oval bodies and large heads with ten irregular tentacles, two of which are very long.

The outer covering of the cuttlefish with the fins has a hard, rough part that must be removed. It is best to wear gloves to do this. The ink sac, if still present, must be removed carefully with the fingers, although it is possible to buy these vacuum-packed in the shops. The ink sac should be kept refrigerated. The ink gives the risotto a distinctive character.

Rice – rich in magnesium and typical of northern Italian cuisine – ranks alongside wheat as the most important source of nutrition in the world. The means by which rice was introduced to the Italian peninsula is disputed. Some historians believe that rice was known to the Romans; others that it was only brought much later to Sicily by the Arabs; and finally the Venetians, who are very proud of their past, insist that it was brought to Italy from the Orient by merchants of the *Serenissima*, the beautiful city of Venice. Whatever its origins, one thing is certain: No rice was cultivated on the Po plain before the 16th century.

Black risotto is a highly original dish and will be very much appreciated by your guests.

Wash the cuttlefish thoroughly under running water. Remove the rough parts and, if necessary, the ink sacs, and set aside. Cut the cuttlefish into small pieces.

Peel and finely chop the onion and cook in a saucepan with 5 tbsp olive oil until soft and transparent. Add the rice and cook for another 2 minutes, stirring constantly.

Gradually add the fish stock to the rice. Simmer for 18 minutes, stirring with a wooden spoon.

Risotto

Heat the remaining olive oil in a pan. Add the cuttlefish and fry until brown. Season with salt and pepper and add the chopped clove of garlic.

Stir the ink into the cuttlefish. Stir with a wooden spoon and add to the rice. Mix very gently.

Sprinkle parmesan over the rice. Stir and add the butter, and adjust seasoning to taste. Serve the risotto garnished with parsley, and cherry tomatoes if desired.

Broccoli

Preparation time:	*35 minutes*
Cooking time:	*50 minutes*
Difficulty:	★★

Serves 4

4 oz/100 g	broccoli
4 oz/100 g	sausagemeat
½	onion
1	dried chile
2 oz/50 g	peeled tomatoes (canned)

4 tbsp	olive oil
	salt
	black pepper
12 oz/300 g	Carnaroli rice
	coarse salt
2 oz/50 g	grated pecorino

Tasty risottos are an integral part of the cuisine of northern Italy, from where they originate. They have now become well known and much loved all over the world. The rice is first fried in olive oil, then butter and parmesan are added. This forms the basis of the dish to which is added the finest regional and seasonal produce, according to individual preference.

Broccoli, a member of the brassica family, is cultivated mainly in southern Italy and is a valuable foodstuff due to its high vitamin and mineral content. As a general rule, only the florets are used; these can be steamed.

Broccoli is available on market stalls in Italy from October to April. When buying broccoli, you should look for dense heads with closed florets that are dark green in color, sometimes with a bluish or purplish tinge. The stalks should be firm. Our chef occasionally substitutes artichokes, which are very popular in her native region, for the broccoli.

The heavily seasoned sausage is what gives the risotto its really powerful flavor. Italian sausages, or *salsiccie* as they are called in Italian, are made from a mixture of lean and fatty pork.

The quality of the risotto is heavily dependent on that of the rice used. There are about 8,000 known varieties of rice, distinguished by the shape of their grains: short, round, medium, or long. The chef recommends using Carnaroli rice, which is large-grained and has a high starch content. This colorful dish should be enhanced with pecorino, a ewe's milk cheese from southern Italy.

Separate the broccoli florets from the stalk. Cook the florets for 10 minutes in a saucepan of boiling, salted water. Remove from the water, drain, and plunge into ice-cold water. Set the cooking liquid aside for later.

Pull the sausages into pieces with your fingers. Peel and finely chop the onion. Cut the chile and the peeled tomatoes into small pieces.

In a saucepan, sauté half the onion, the sausagemeat, and the tomatoes in 1 tbsp olive oil for about 5 minutes. Add the broccoli, season with salt and pepper, and cook for another 5 minutes.

Risotto

In another pan, sauté the remaining onion with the chile in the rest of the olive oil. Add the rice and continue to sauté, stirring with a wooden spoon.

Pour 2 cups/500 ml of the reserved cooking liquid over the rice and simmer for 20 minutes, stirring constantly.

Carefully fold the broccoli mixture into the rice. Leave to infuse for 5 minutes and season with coarse salt to taste. Sprinkle with grated pecorino and serve the risotto hot.

Porcini Mushroom Risotto

Preparation time: 15 minutes
Soaking time: 1 hour
Cooking time: 25 minutes
Difficulty: ☆

Serves 4

⅓ cup/40 g	dried porcini mushrooms
4 tbsp	olive oil
2	onions
1½ cups/ 300 g	Vialone-Nano rice (or other risotto rice)
7 tbsp	white wine

1 lb/400 g	pumpkin
	salt
1 clove	garlic
½ bunch	parsley
½ tsp/3 g	ground saffron
	pepper
2oz/50 g	grated parmesan

For the garnish:

parsley
dried saffron strands

Although the home of risotto is in northern Italy, more specifically Milan, the rest of Italy has also mastered the art of cooking rice. It is fried in oil and combined with local produce, which almost invariably includes butter and parmesan. This porcini mushroom risotto is a well-known specialty of the Marche region. The natives of the Marche region have a reputation for being fond of the pleasures of the table, especially rice dishes.

Alberto Melagrana specifically recommends the Vialone-Nano variety of rice, the grains of which are rather fat, quite firm, and have a high starch content. If you cook the rice in vegetable stock instead of water, the risotto will have an even more piquant flavor.

Saffron is a much sought-after spice and is cultivated in the province of L'Aquila in the Abruzzi region. According to some historians, the Romans were admirers of this valuable plant, using it, among other things, to scent their theaters. Saffron was also used as a strong yellow dye for silk.

The inhabitants of L'Aquila, who traded with Venice, Milan, and Marseille, concentrated on growing saffron in the Middle Ages. Saffron from this region is still highly prized throughout Italy today. In our recipe, the powdered saffron must be dissolved in a little water before use.

Alberto Melagrana loves porcini mushrooms. They are recognizable by their club-shaped stalk and convex heads. According to our chef, the unmistakable taste of porcini mushrooms is ideal for a risotto flavored with saffron.

The addition of creamed pumpkin gives this dish its unique sophistication.

Soak the dried porcini mushrooms for 1 hour in water. Heat 2 tbsp olive oil in a copper saucepan. Sauté 1 chopped onion until soft and transparent, then add the rice and sauté, stirring constantly, until it, too, is soft and transparent.

Add the white wine. When it has reduced, slowly pour in 2½ cups/600 ml water. Simmer for about 15 minutes.

Peel the pumpkin and cut into cubes. Transfer the pumpkin and the remaining peeled onion to a saucepan, add a glass of water, cover, and simmer for 15 minutes. Strain, and purée the pumpkin and onion. Season with salt.

with Creamed Pumpkin

Sauté the whole peeled garlic clove in a pan with 1 tbsp olive oil. Add the diced mushrooms and cook slowly. Stir in the chopped parsley.

Add the mushroom mixture to the rice. Dissolve the ground saffron in half a glass of water and pour into the rice. Season with salt and pepper.

Remove the pan from the stove and sprinkle the grated parmesan over the top. Add 1 tbsp olive oil. Transfer the creamed pumpkin and risotto onto plates and serve garnished with parsley and saffron threads.

Spaghetti with

Preparation time:	20 minutes
Cooking time:	30 minutes
Difficulty:	☆

Serves 4

3¼ lb/1.5 kg	small langoustines
1	shallot
7 tbsp	olive oil
	salt
4 tbsp	dry champagne

4	tomatoes
¼	green bell pepper
1lb/400 g	spaghetti alla chitarra (or ordinary spaghetti)

For the garnish:

| | strips of green bell pepper |

Every region in Italy has its own variety of pasta. In Abruzzi and Molise, the typical spaghetti is *alla chitarra*, named after the "guitar" (*chitarra* in Italian) that is used to prepare this particular kind of pasta. *Spaghetti alla chitarra* is usually served with meat, but our chef recommends using langoustines instead in this recipe.

The ingenious inventor of the *chitarra*, unfortunately unknown, was undoubtedly a music- as well as a pasta-lover, and would certainly be a household name in Abruzzi and Molise were his identity known.

The *chitarra*, which is indispensable when making spaghetti and macaroni, consists of a rectangular beechwood frame across which very fine metal wires are stretched at regular intervals of ¹⁄₂₅ inch/1 millimeter. Just as in a real guitar, the strings can be tightened up with a special key when they become slack. The pasta dough is pressed onto the *chitarra*, which cuts it into very fine rectangular strips. You can, however, use ordinary spaghetti or macaroni.

Langoustines are found in abundance off the coasts of western Europe. They resemble small lobsters or large shrimp, either of which can be substituted for the langoustines in this recipe. Langoustines are very popular because of their outstanding meat and are available all year round. When you buy them, make sure they still have their claws, their shells are shiny, and that they still have the characteristic smell of the sea, with its tang of iodine.

This dish is pasta at its most sublime!

Twist off the heads of the langoustines and remove the meat from the shells. Reserve the meat and heads (with claws). Place the shells in a saucepan with 8 cups/2 liters water, boil for 30 minutes. Strain the stock and set aside.

Peel the shallot and chop finely. Sauté with olive oil in a pan. Add the langoustine meat and heads and sauté for 3 minutes. Season with salt.

Pour on the champagne and reduce for 5 minutes. Wash the tomatoes, then blanch, skin, and chop them finely. Cut the bell pepper into thin strips.

Langoustines

Add the diced tomatoes and bell pepper to the pan, cover, and cook slowly for about 5 minutes.

Bring the strained langoustine stock to the boil and season with salt. Add the spaghetti and boil until cooked "al dente." Remove from the water and drain the spaghetti.

Add the spaghetti immediately to the seafood and stir well. Serve on plates with strips of green bell pepper.

Spaghetti

Preparation time:	20 minutes
Cooking time:	25 minutes
Difficulty:	★

Serves 4

1 clove	garlic
7 tbsp	extra-virgin olive oil
3 oz/80 g	anchovies in oil
½ cup/60 g	black olives
8 oz/200 g	cherry tomatoes

1⅓ cup/40 g	capers
8 oz/200 g	spaghetti
	salt
	olive oil
1	small chile

Guests at the "Taverna del Capitano" restaurant in Marina del Cantone, near Naples, have a heavenly view over the Gulf of Naples and the island of Capri. In his restaurant, Alfonso Caputo likes to serve spaghetti with a sauce made from cherry tomatoes, anchovies, capers, garlic, and chile – a traditional Italian dish.

To enhance his recipe further, the chef recommends using handmade pasta. The spaghetti he prefers is around 22 inches/55 centimeters long and has an uneven, beige-white color. The spaghetti is hung up to dry before it is cut, which is why the ends are curled. They have to be broken in the middle to fit in the saucepan. Alfonso Caputo does not drain his pasta in a sieve, but removes it from the water using a spaghetti spoon, shakes it briefly over the saucepan, and transfers it immediately to the pan containing the sauce.

Anchovies are among the fish caught off the coast of Naples and are brought out of the water at night. For this recipe, Alfonso Caputo uses canned anchovies in oil.

Cherry tomatoes are grown on a large scale in Corbara, near Naples. Their acidic, not very sweet taste goes perfectly with fish and seafood. These decorative, tasty fruit are best eaten in a sauce or on a pizza.

The powerful taste of the capers gives the sauce its characteristic flavor. Capers are the closed flower buds of the caper bush, a shrub commonly found on the stony soil of the Italian coast. They are gathered in spring and preserved in brine to remove any bitterness. The best capers are said to grow on the islands of Lipari and Pantelleria off the Sicilian coast.

Peel the garlic and chop finely. Heat the olive oil in a skillet and sauté the garlic for 2–3 minutes. Add the anchovies and infuse for 4–5 minutes.

Pit the olives and chop coarsely.

Wash and dry the tomatoes, then cut them into quarters.

del Capitano

Add the capers, chopped olives, and tomatoes to the anchovies in the pan. Simmer for 5 minutes.

Boil the spaghetti in salted water until it is just "al dente," then remove from the water with a spaghetti spoon, drain, and add to the sauce. Infuse for 5 minutes, stirring the sauce frequently.

Season with a dash of olive oil and small pieces of chile. Serve immediately.

Spinosini with

Preparation time:	20 minutes
Cooking time:	15 minutes
Difficulty:	★

Serves 4

4 oz/100 g	broccoli florets
3 oz/80 g	black truffles
8 tbsp	olive oil
1 clove	garlic
1	anchovy fillet

2 oz/50 g	pitted black olives
2 oz/50 g	cherry tomatoes
10 oz/250 g	spinosini (or ordinary spaghetti)
	coarse salt
	pepper

For the garnish:

| | truffle shavings |

In Italy there are as many types of pasta as there are ways of preparing it. Pasta enjoys a status similar to that of soccer, and both are the subjects of passionate arguments. In a country in which pasta is revered, each province claims that it is the birthplace of pasta, marrying it in true ceremonial style with the best produce of the particular region.

Spinosini resembles long, thin spaghetti and is typical of the Campo Filone region. This excellent egg pasta is made using a cherrywood board, which gives it a characteristic flavor. According to the chef, *spinosini* has properties that make it very good for cooking, but traditional spaghetti can also be used in this recipe.

In the Marche region, *spinosini* is traditionally eaten in winter with goulash, while in hot weather it is served with tomatoes and basil. Alberto Melagrana recommends combining *spinosini* with black truffles. This mushroom, which grows underground, is highly regarded in the province of Pesaro, the native city of composer Gioacchino Rossini. Even in ancient times, the Roman gourmet Apicius described the truffle as "the acme of luxury." Like his contemporaries, he believed that truffles only grew under trees that had been struck by lightning by Jupiter, the god who ruled the forces of nature. When buying truffles, the chef recommends that you look for round, firm ones. If you want to keep them for a few days, they can be wrapped individually in parchment and stored in an airtight container in a cool place.

Broccoli originates from southern Italy and is rich in vitamin C and minerals. It is available from October to April, but its close relative cauliflower can be substituted in this recipe if required.

Separate the broccoli florets from the stalk using a knife. Boil the florets for 5 minutes in salted water.

Remove the broccoli from the saucepan and plunge into ice water. Remove after a few minutes and drain.

Grate the black truffles. For the sauce, heat 3 tbsp olive oil in a pan with an unpeeled clove of garlic. Add the grated truffles. Sauté briefly and set aside.

Black Truffles

Pour the remaining oil into a pan and sauté the washed, finely chopped anchovy, finely diced olives and tomatoes, and broccoli florets for 1 minute.

Heat some water in a large saucepan and boil the spinosini until cooked "al dente," then remove from the water and drain.

Transfer the pasta to the pan with the broccoli. Fry briefly, then season to taste with coarse salt and pepper. Serve on plates with the truffle sauce, garnished with truffle shavings.

Trenette

Preparation time: 15 minutes
Cooking time: 20 minutes
Difficulty: ✫

Serves 4

3	potatoes
8 oz/200 g	green beans
1¼ lb/500 g	trenette (pasta)
	salt

For the pesto:

3 cloves	garlic
⅓ cup/40 g	pine nuts

1 heaped tsp/ 6 g	coarse salt
5 bunches	basil
1 cup/120 g	grated parmesan
¼ cup/30 g	grated pecorino
8 tbsp	olive oil

For the garnish:

pine nuts
basil leaves

Anyone who has ever been to Genoa will remember the winding narrow streets in the old town and certainly also the scent of fresh basil drifting out of the kitchen windows. In this Ligurian city, the matriarchs are indisputably the best pesto makers in the whole world! Pesto goes especially well with *trenette*, long pasta made from wheat flour, which is eaten with potatoes and green beans.

Pesto means "crushed." Genoese pesto consists basically of basil, olive oil, garlic, parmesan, and pecorino. The addition of pine nuts is a contentious issue; purists are firmly opposed to the use of pine nuts, as they say this is a variant that originated in Savona. Others, such as Marco and Rosella Folicaldi, insist that the long seeds of the umbrella pine should definitely be included in the ingredients of this original recipe.

The method used to prepare pesto is also a contentious issue. One of the long-disputed questions is whether it is necessary to wash the basil. This disagreement between the experts actually conceals a real problem: whether it is possible to make a genuine Genoese pesto using a blender instead of the famous marble mortar and olive wood pestle. The matriarchs of Genoa, who painstakingly crush the ingredients with a pestle and mortar, would naturally answer this question with a resounding "No!"

The gourmets are in agreement about one point at least: The quality of the olive oil is crucial to the quality of the pesto. For this reason, it is best to use extra-virgin olive oil. In their – often tiny – gardens, Ligurians prefer to grow a variety of basil with small leaves, which has a heavenly fragrance.

For the pesto, mix together the peeled garlic cloves, pine nuts, and coarse salt in a blender.

Add the basil leaves, grated cheeses, and olive oil, and blend into a homogeneous sauce. Set the pesto aside.

Peel the potatoes, cut into pieces, and boil for 10 minutes in salted water.

with Pesto

Wash the green beans and remove the stalks. Add to the pan of potatoes and boil for about 2 minutes.

Add the trenette and boil until "al dente."

Carefully stir the drained pasta with the potatoes and beans into the pesto. Transfer to plates and garnish with pine nuts and basil leaves.

Fish & Seafood

Eel

Preparation time:	30 minutes
Marinating:	24 hours
Cooking time:	1 hour 20 minutes
Difficulty:	★★

Serves 4

2¼ lb/1 kg	eels
1 stick	celery
3	onions
14	bay leaves

	peppercorns
7 tbsp	white wine
	salt
1 cup/250 ml	extra-virgin olive oil
1¼ lb /500 g	tomatoes
	pepper

Trieste lies on the northern Adriatic coast along a narrow strip of coastline near the Slovenian and Croatian borders. The Istrians have the most delicious ways of cooking eels, as these are in plentiful supply in the estuaries and still waters of the numerous lagoons.

The eel is an extraordinary fish, resembling a snake. It grows up to 3 feet/1 meter in length. Eels hatch in the Sargasso Sea near Bermuda, and the larvae then migrate to Europe, assisted by the Gulf Stream – a journey that takes two to three years. On arrival, they swim upriver, where they grow to sexual maturity. They then swim back to the sea to return to their breeding grounds, with fishermen taking this opportunity to catch them.

You can buy fresh eels from the fishmongers, who kill and skin them. Be sure to check how fresh the eels are (they should have been killed on the day they are sold), as eel meat can spoil very quickly. Eels are also sold canned, frozen or smoked.

You should marinate eel meat for a day in a mixture of white wine and vegetables. The acid in the alcohol "precooks" the flesh slightly so that it absorbs the flavors of the vegetables. This part of the process is not essential, however, and you can cook the eels just as they are.

In Istria, eels are braised in the same pan as the tomatoes and onions, but Paolo Zoppolatti cooks the fish and vegetables separately so that he can pour off the fish fat. This results in a more balanced flavor.

Obtain eels that have been prepared.

On a chopping board, cut the eel into pieces the length of your finger.

Transfer the pieces of eel to a glass, ovenproof dish. Add the coarsely chopped celery, half an onion (sliced), 4 bay leaves, and a few peppercorns, and pour in the white wine. Cover and marinate for 24 hours in the refrigerator.

Istrian Style

The next day, remove the pieces of eel from the marinade and season with salt. Put ¾ cup/200 ml olive oil in a skillet and heat until it is very hot. Fry the fish for about 10 minutes, then keep warm.

Chop the remaining onions finely. Put the rest of the oil in another skillet and fry the onions, tomatoes (cut into strips), and 2 bay leaves over high heat for 5 minutes. Add a little water, then season with salt and pepper. Simmer for another 3–4 minutes over medium heat.

Pass the sauce through a sieve. Transfer some of the tomato mixture to each plate and pour over a little of the sauce. Top with 3 pieces of eel and garnish with 2 bay leaves.

Dried Cod

Preparation time: 30 minutes
Desalting
  the fish: 48 hours
Soaking time: 1 hour
Cooking time: 35 minutes
Difficulty: ★

Serves 4

12 oz/300 g	dried cod (stockfish)
2 tbsp/30 g	currants
2	onions
8 oz/200 g	potatoes
3 cups/750 ml	milk

	pepper
4 tsp/20 g	pine nuts
8 oz/200 g	Swiss chard leaves
	olive oil

For the piquant sauce (optional):
Blend together:

2	red chiles, chopped and de-seeded
1 tbsp	paprika
3 tbsp	olive oil

The traditional recipes of the Marche region, the home of Alberto Melagrana, continually provide him with new inspiration so that he is forever passionately creating unusual new recipes. At "Il Furlo," his restaurant in Aqualagna, whose sign dates back to 1888, he works mostly with regional produce.

Baccalà, as the Italians call cod that has been preserved in salt, no longer plays a very important part in cooking in the countryside, although villagers used to travel to the Adriatic coast twice a year to stock up with this fish, which was very valuable as it could be kept for such a long time. Dried cod from Norway is very popular in Spain and especially in Portugal. Its lean, tasty flesh can be prepared in many different ways, but it is essential to soak it in water for 48 hours to get rid of the salt.

Seedless currants taste sweet and are often used for cooking in southern Italy, but they must be soaked in water for an hour beforehand. They are a delicious source of energy.

In this springtime dish, the fish is wrapped in Swiss chard leaves. Swiss chard is rich in vitamins A and C. Its leaves, which are rather less tender and mild than spinach, must be washed thoroughly before use.

The ramekins should be oiled before being lined with the Swiss chard, and covered with aluminum foil after filling.

Surprise your guests with this unusual dish!

Cover the dried cod with water and soak for 48 hours to remove the salt, changing the water several times. Soak the currants in water in a small bowl for 1 hour.

Bone the cod using tweezers and remove any skin etc. with a knife. Briefly blanch the peeled onions twice in boiling water, changing the water in between.

Peel the potatoes and cook with the onions in 2 cups/500 ml milk for about 20 minutes. Season with pepper. Cream together in a blender and set aside.

"Il Furlo"

Cut the dried cod into pieces and place in a saucepan with the remaining milk. Roast the pine nuts in a skillet without any fat.

Add the soaked currants to the dried cod and simmer for 20 minutes. Add the pine nuts. Blanch the Swiss chard leaves for 2 minutes in boiling water, then cool by plunging into cold water. Oil the ramekins.

Line the ramekins with Swiss chard leaves, place the fish inside, and fold the leaves over the top. Cook for 15 minutes in a bain-marie or double boiler. Place some creamed potato on each plate with a portion of fish in the center. Serve with a drizzle of piquant sauce, if desired.

Dried Cod Frecole

Preparation time: 30 minutes
Desalting
   the fish: 48 hours
Cooking time: 20 minutes
Difficulty: ★

Serves 4

1¼ lb/500 g	dried cod (stockfish)
1⅓ cups/	
150 g	walnut kernels
10 oz/250 g	stale bread
1 clove	garlic

2 tsp/10 g	dried oregano
	salt (optional)
	pepper
3 tbsp	olive oil

For the garnish:

	walnuts
	oregano leaves

The word *frecole* is Italian dialect for the crumb of a loaf of bread, which in this region is often used instead of fine breadcrumbs. This typical, dried-cod dish from Avellino is traditional Christmas fare.

Cod, which is highly regarded by other nations as well as the Italians, is one of the most frequently caught fish worldwide. In Norway, it is made into dried cod: In other words, it is cut into two and heavily salted before being left to dry in the open air. It is therefore absolutely essential to soak it thoroughly for 48 hours before use.

Thanks to its lean, tasty flesh, *baccalà*, as the Italians call dried cod, is a gourmet food. In this recipe, it is possible to substitute sole or gold bream, in which case Michelina Fischetti recommends that you add tomatoes and parsley to round off the dish.

The *frecole* mixture consists of garlic, oregano, olive oil, and walnuts. The nuts give the dish bite, as well as being healthy and nutritious. Walnuts should always be kept in an airtight container in a cool, dry place. In order to "rejuvenate" them, soak them for a few hours in hot milk. The skins will then fall off practically by themselves and the nuts will be fresh and crunchy again. You can of course use filberts or almonds as an alternative.

Oregano is a wild variety of marjoram with a rather stronger taste. It is indispensable in Italian cookery, especially as a seasoning in many tomato dishes.

Dried cod *frecole* is an excellent dish for festive occasions, not just at Christmas time.

Using a large knife, cut the dried cod into even-sized pieces and remove the bones.

Lay the pieces of fish in a bowl of water. Soak the fish for 48 hours to remove the salt, changing the water several times.

Crush the walnuts with a pestle and mortar.

with Nuts

Rub the bread into crumbs with your hands. Peel and crush the garlic.

Place the breadcrumbs, garlic, oregano, and crushed walnuts in a salad bowl. Season with salt (if desired) and pepper. Add 2 tbsp olive oil and combine the ingredients, using your hands.

Oil an ovenproof dish with 1 tbsp olive oil, place the fish in it, and sprinkle over the nut mixture. Bake in the oven for 20 minutes at 350° F/180° C. Serve garnished with whole walnuts and a few oregano leaves.

Brodetto

Preparation time: 1 hour
Cooking time: 50 minutes
Difficulty: ★

Serves 4

1 lb/400 g	monkfish
1¾ lb/800 g	herring
2	sole, each 8 oz/200 g
2	medium-sized red mullet
2	gurnard
1¼ lb/500 g	ray
6	tomatoes

4 tbsp	olive oil
1 clove	garlic
½	green bell pepper
2	cuttlefish, each 8 oz/200 g
	salt
4	medium-sized langoustines
4	gray shrimp
1	red chile (optional)

For the garnish:

parsley

In Italian cookery, the term *brodetto* signifies a fish soup. There are countless regional variations on this dish: In the Marche region, up to 13 different kinds of fish are used, and seafood is added as well!

Maddalena Beccaceci, who comes from Abruzzi, has devised a *brodetto* here that bears some resemblance to *bouillabaisse*. It is traditionally cooked in a *tajine*, an earthenware casserole, and eaten with toasted bread. This recipe, with tomatoes, green pepper, garlic, and olive oil, includes a variety of fish from the Mediterranean, the Adriatic, and the Atlantic. It is easy to prepare and has the major advantage that it can be varied according to the availability of the ingredients at the market or as personal taste dictates.

Maddalena cooks some fish, such as red mullet (red snapper can be used instead) and gurnard, whole. Both are highly sought-after because of their lean, white flesh.

When buying, make sure that the fish are fresh, the eyes are bright and not sunken, and that the scales are shiny.

Herring is a particularly fine fish. It is flecked with black and grows to a length of 12–16 inches/30–40 centimeters. Just 40 percent of its weight consists of firm, succulent flesh, which is easy to remove from the bones. Take special care when cleaning this fish, as it has very prickly fins.

Ray should be soaked in water containing vinegar for a few minutes to make it easy to remove the slime from the skin. It needs cooking for a long time and tastes best hot.

Lovers of langoustine will also enjoy this dish – its delicate flesh adds extra flavor to this sumptuous fish soup.

Preparing the fish: Skin the monkfish and cut into medallions. Gut the herring, sole, red mullet, and gurnard, and remove the scales. Skin the sole. Cut the ray and the herring into pieces.

Blanch, skin, and dice the tomatoes. Oil a high-sided baking sheet, place the chopped garlic in it, place the sheet over heat and sauté the garlic. Lay the tomatoes and finely chopped green bell pepper on the sheet and sauté for about 5 minutes.

Add the prepared and cleaned cuttlefish, cut into small pieces. Season with salt, then cover the baking sheet with aluminum foil and cook for 5 minutes.

alla Beccaceci

Add the herring, the monkfish medallions, and the ray. Cover again and cook for another 5 minutes over low heat.

Carefully add the sole, red mullet, and gurnard. Cover and cook for 3–4 minutes.

Add the langoustines and shrimp, and chile (chopped and de-seeded) if desired. Cover again and cook for a further 5 minutes. Transfer the Brodetto alla Beccaceci onto plates and sprinkle with chopped parsley.

Cacciucco

Preparation time: *1 hour*
Cooking time: *55 minutes*
Difficulty: ★★

Serves 4

8 oz/200 g	eel
8 oz/200 g	salmon trout
4	live crayfish
12 oz/320 g	swordfish
1	small, dried chile
	olive oil
1 clove	garlic
1 tbsp	chopped parsley
1 scant cup/	
200 ml	white wine

11 oz/300g	tomatoes
	salt
	pepper

For the fish stock:

	head, bones, and fins of the trout
1	small stick celery
½	carrot
½	onion
3	basil leaves
	salt

To serve:

toasted slices of
   farmhouse bread
extra-virgin olive oil
chopped parsley

The Serchio river, with its plentiful supply of fish and crustaceans, flows past Sauro Brunicardi's restaurant, "La Mora." This has given the chef the idea of transforming a traditional recipe from Livorno, on the coast of the Tyrrhenian Sea, and adapting it to use freshwater fish from the Serchio. Legend has it that, a long time ago, a poor widow from Livorno used to beg for the waste from fish and mollusks in order to make a thin soup, which is how *cacciucco* originated. With time, the list of ingredients grew somewhat, to include fish from the region as well as crustaceans. The tasty sauce in this *cacciucco* consists of tomatoes, garlic, parsley, white wine, and herbs.

With the exception of the swordfish, the fish used by Sauro Brunicardi are mainly freshwater fish. Freshwater fish are seldom eaten in Italy, because their flesh is considered insipid, but eels are certainly an exception to this. They are caught in southern Tuscany in the Bay of Orbetello when they swim down the Albegna River toward the sea.

When you buy fresh eels, make sure that they have been killed and prepared by the fishmonger on the day of purchase; they should be as fresh as possible. Eels are also sold smoked, canned or frozen.

When preparing the salmon trout, be sure to remove all the bones, or ask the fishmonger to fillet it for you. Sauro Brunicardi serves his *cacciucco* with Tuscan bread baked in wood-fired ovens, which has a very firm crust. The bread is first toasted and then drizzled with oil; it is wonderful for soaking up the sauce.

Obtain prepared eel. Cut the eel into pieces 1–1½ in/3–4 cm long.

Make a cut along the lower edge and gut the salmon trout. Slice along the backbone and make a horizontal cut just above the tail. Run the knife along the backbone to loosen the fillets. Cut these into strips 1½–2 in/4–5 cm wide and 4 in/10 cm long.

Place the head, bones, and fins of the salmon trout in a saucepan of salted water. Add the celery, carrot, peeled onion, basil, and salt to taste. Simmer for 30 minutes over low heat. Strain and set aside.

Add the crayfish to a pan of bubbling boiling water and cook for 2 minutes. Cut along them lengthways. Slice the swordfish. Cut the chile and remove the seeds.

Fry the peeled and sliced garlic in oil in a large skillet. Add the parsley and finely chopped chile and sauté for 1 minute. Add the swordfish, eel, crayfish, and salmon trout and cook for 5 minutes, stirring constantly. Quench with white wine.

Add the chopped tomatoes and cook for 5 minutes over high heat. Season with salt and pepper. Pour over the fish stock and simmer for 10 minutes. Transfer the fish, crayfish, sauce, and the slices of bread drizzled with olive oil onto plates and garnish with chopped parsley.

Jumbo Shrimp with

Preparation time: 10 minutes
Soaking time: 12 hours
Cooking time: 1 hour
Difficulty: ★

Serves 4

2 cups/ 400 g	cannellini (white kidney) beans
1	bay leaf
1	carrot
1	stick celery

1	onion
4 tbsp	olive oil
1	tomato or 4 cherry tomatoes
12	jumbo shrimp
½ bunch	parsley
	salt
	pepper

The Italian Adriatic coast is famous for the wonderful seafood dishes that are prepared there. In Vicenza, the native city of Francesca de Giovannini, jumbo shrimp (also known as king prawns) are a favorite, traditionally eaten with polenta.

The chef has made some changes to this traditional recipe: Instead of polenta, she serves the shrimp with a cream made from beans.

Jumbo shrimp are highly prized due to their extremely tender flesh. They are usually steamed, as this method of cooking preserves their unique flavor. Depending on availability, you can substitute smaller-sized shrimp.

The Italians are extremely fond of dried beans. Of the many varieties, the white, kidney-shaped cannellini beans deserve a special mention. These originate from Tuscany,

but are now found throughout Italy. They are highly nutritious and contain many vitamins. Soak them in water for 12 hours before use. The chef occasionally substitutes a mousse made from garbanzo beans or fava beans for the creamed beans.

This dish is greatly enhanced by the typical Mediterranean sauce containing olive oil, parsley, salt, and pepper, which brings out the flavor of the crustaceans even more. Parsley is available all year round and is sometimes used in large quantities in order to counter the strong flavor provided by certain ingredients.

Treat yourself and your guests to these wonderfully delicious jumbo shrimp!

Soak the dried beans in water with the bay leaf, the peeled and sliced carrot, celery, and onion, cut into chunks, for 12 hours.

Transfer the drained beans and vegetables to a saucepan and boil for about 1 hour in salted water.

Purée the cooked beans in a blender, then add 2 tbsp olive oil.

Creamed Beans

Blanch, skin, and dice the tomatoes. If using cherry tomatoes, halve them.

Steam the jumbo shrimp for 4–5 minutes, then remove the meat from the shells.

For the sauce, mix together 2 tbsp olive oil, chopped parsley, salt, and pepper. Transfer the jumbo shrimp to plates with the tomatoes and the creamed beans. Pour over a little of the sauce and serve.

Stuffed

Preparation time: 45 minutes
Cooking time: 45 minutes
Difficulty: ★★

Serves 4

2 lb/800 g	cuttlefish
6 oz/150 g	sliced bread
9 tbsp	extra-virgin olive oil
1¼ lb/500 g	cherry tomatoes
1	small chile
1 clove	garlic
	salt
1 scant cup/ 200 ml	rosé wine

The "Taverna del Capitano" in the Bay of Naples is the restaurant of Alfonso Caputo, who has made a specialty of fish and seafood dishes. When preparing stuffed cuttlefish, the filling traditionally consists of the tentacles, minced pork or veal, and sliced bread. The chef suggests a lighter filling, however, mixing the tentacles with cherry tomatoes, bread cubes, garlic, and chile.

Cuttlefish belong to the cephalopod family and are classed as marine mollusks. They have a dark skin, but their flesh is tender and extremely tasty. They are fished from the depths of the sea, using dragnets and are a particular favorite of Neapolitan cooks, who either stuff them or serve them in soups or with pasta. Sliced bread is the perfect filling. After you have carefully removed the crusts, stack the slices of bread on top of one another and cut into cubes. The strong, red color and mildly acidic flavor of the cherry tomatoes make a huge contribution to the suc-

cess of this dish. They go extremely well with both the cuttlefish and the subtle acidity of the rosé wine used for cooking. Alfonso Caputo recommends a Lacrima Christi from Campagna, but any other rosé wine, or even white wine, can be used.

Cooking the cuttlefish so that the outside and the filling are equally tender is the only difficulty with this recipe. When the sauce has reduced and started to thicken, the cuttlefish are just right. Cut through them carefully, so that the filling does not fall out of the outer rings. Place three medallions and a little sauce on each plate and then garnish with a little chopped parsley.

Cut off the heads of the cuttlefish and remove the innards. Pull off the skin and rinse thoroughly under running water.

Dice the tentacles. Cut the bread into small cubes.

Heat 2 tbsp olive oil in a pan and fry the tentacles. Add half the cherry tomatoes, the bread cubes, the finely sliced chile, and the sliced garlic. Cook over high heat.

Cuttlefish

Add the cuttlefish to the pan. Spoon in the filling and seal with a wooden skewer.

Pour the remaining olive oil into an oven-proof dish. Add the remaining cherry tomatoes and season with salt. Lay the cuttlefish in the dish and pour over the wine. Arrange the remaining filling around the cuttlefish and cover the dish with aluminum foil. Bake in the oven for 40 minutes at 340° F/170° C.

When the cuttlefish and stuffing are both cooked, set aside in a warm place. Sieve and purée the vegetables from the baking dish, using some of the liquor, sufficient to make a smooth sauce. Slice the cuttle-fish into 3 rings and arrange on plates in the sauce. Serve very hot.

Red Mullet Fillet

Preparation time:	40 minutes	
Resting time for		
the polenta:	1 hour	
Cooking time:	10 minutes	
Difficulty:	☆	

Serves 4

4	red mullet, each 8 oz/200 g
12	cherry tomatoes
	salt
	pepper
4 tbsp	sunflower oil

For the nut pesto:

8 oz/200 g	walnut kernels
2 cloves	garlic
1½ oz/40 g	fresh basil
1⅔ cups/ 400 ml	olive oil
	salt
	pepper

For the polenta:

2 cups/500 ml	milk
½ stick/60 g	butter
⅔ cup/100 g	cornmeal
	salt
	pepper

World-famous *pesto genovese* is made with basil and pine nuts, and eaten with pasta. Here, Sergio Pais introduces his own variation on this classic dish. Instead of pine nuts he uses walnuts and, being a fish lover, serves his pesto with red mullet fillets, which are highly regarded in Liguria.

Red mullet, with its characteristic three scales beneath the eyes, was popular even in ancient times. Its firm, tasty flesh requires only brief cooking. Even if the fishmonger has filleted the fish for you, do not forget to remove any remaining small bones with tweezers. Depending on availability, you can substitute red snapper, gold bream or herring for the red mullet.

In Ligurian cooking, walnuts are used mainly for *salsa dei noci*, a nut sauce. Walnuts originated in Asia and were introduced to Italy by the Romans in ancient times.

The most important ingredient in any pesto is the basil, with its strong fragrance and brilliant green color. A particularly fine-tasting variety of basil flourishes in the gardens of Genoa. This aromatic plant is an import from India and its name is derived from the ancient Greek word *basilikos*, meaning "royal." In the kitchen, basil is added mainly to tomato and pasta dishes.

These red mullet fillets are served with polenta. Polenta is a specialty from the Veneto region that is now available all over northern Italy. Culinary purists still cook polenta over wood fires, then cut it on a wooden board using the wetted blunt edge of a knife.

For the polenta, heat the milk, add the butter, and pour in the cornmeal. Stir with a wooden spatula and cook for 3–4 minutes. Season with salt and pepper.

Spread out a damp dish cloth and spread the polenta on it. Fold up the cloth securely and leave to stand for 1 hour.

Remove the scales from the mullet and cut into the fin. Make a cut from the head along the backbone as far as the tail. Turn the fish over and repeat the process on the other side. Cut off the fillets and remove the small bones. Make an indentation in the fillets at one end.

with Nut Pesto

For the pesto, mix the walnuts, garlic, basil leaves, and olive oil in a blender and season to taste with salt and pepper.

Lay the fish fillets in a skillet, skin side down. Brush the fillets with pesto. Add the halved cherry tomatoes. Season with salt and pepper. Bake in the oven for 3 minutes at 350° F/180° C (if necessary, unscrew the skillet handle beforehand).

Unwrap the polenta and cut into regular slices. Pour the sunflower oil into a pan and fry the polenta slices until golden yellow. Season with salt and pepper. Serve the fish fillets with polenta and some of the pesto.

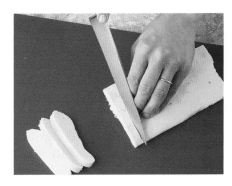

Turbot Fillet

Preparation time:	*20 minutes*
Cooking time:	*1 hour 15 minutes*
Difficulty:	✶✶

Serves 4

salt	
1¼ cups/ 200 g	white cornmeal
1	turbot weighing 2¼–2¾ lb/1–1.2 kg
2 cloves	garlic
6 tbsp	extra-virgin olive oil
1½ tbsp	white wine vinegar pepper

1 scant cup/ 200 ml	white wine salt

To serve:

	coarse ground black pepper

We owe *boreto*, a fish sauce, consisting of vinegar, white wine, black pepper, and garlic, to the fishermen of Friuli and Venezia Giulia. It is used to enhance eel, turbot, and perch dishes. Paolo Zoppolatti serves his turbot in *boreto* on a bed of white polenta.

Turbot, with its lozenge-shaped body, is found both in the Atlantic and the Mediterranean. With its tender, succulent white flesh, it is one of the finest fish. Our chef recommends frying the fillets briefly before pouring the *boreto* over them.

White polenta, which has a more subtle flavor than the yellow variety, is very popular in Friuli as an accompaniment to broiled or fried fish. Since the 17th century, when corn was introduced by Venetian merchants, this sumptuous dish has numbered among the culinary treasures of the Adriatic region.

Paolo Zoppolatti uses classic cornmeal, which means that 40–45 minutes are required for preparation. Pre-cooked polenta, which is ready in 20 minutes, however, is also available. Polenta is traditionally cooked in a copper cauldron over a wood fire (copper is a very good conductor of heat). The water must be heated until it is nearly boiling. In order to determine whether it has reached the correct temperature, test with a pinch of cornmeal: If a whirlpool is formed, then the rest of the cornmeal can be added. Stir well with a wooden spoon, constantly reversing direction, until the consistency of thick oatmeal porridge has been reached. To make the polenta smoother, cook the cornmeal in a mixture of milk and water.

To serve, you can add a little olive oil to bind the fish sauce. Garnish the fish with a few fried cherry tomatoes.

In a saucepan, bring 3½ cups/800 ml salted water to just under boiling point. Add the cornmeal and cook for 40 minutes, stirring constantly, until the consistency of thick oatmeal porridge is reached.

Cut open the turbot along the backbone and fillet it. Chop the bones and the other off-cuts of the fish.

Fry the peeled, halved garlic cloves in 2 tbsp olive oil in a skillet. Add the bones and other off-cuts of the fish, remove the garlic, and fry over high heat for 5 minutes.

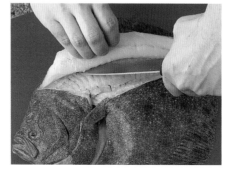

with Polenta

Add the vinegar and scrape around the bottom of the pan with a wooden spatula to incorporate all the browned ingredients. Season with pepper. Reduce over medium heat for 5 minutes.

Quench with white wine, scrape the bottom of the pan again, and add some water. Reduce for another 10 minutes, season with salt, then strain.

Season the turbot fillets with salt. Fry in the remaining olive oil for 5 minutes on each side. Serve each fillet on a bed of polenta, pour the fish sauce all round, and sprinkle with ground black pepper.

Venus Clams

Preparation time:	10 minutes
Cooking time:	40 minutes
Difficulty:	★

Serves 4

4 sprigs	rosemary
4	fresh porcini mushrooms
12	shelled Venus clams
4 slices	fatty bacon
	salt
	pepper
2 tbsp	vegetable oil
2 tbsp	white wine

For the cornmeal cream:

	coarse salt
1¼ cups/	
200 g	cornmeal
½ bunch	fresh chives

For the garnish:

	rosemary sprigs

This recipe, created by Francesca de Giovannini, is a particularly sophisticated hot appetizer. The Venus clam kebabs are easy to prepare and are served with creamed cornmeal, a special kind of polenta.

Venus clams, which are found in coastal waters, are extremely popular because of their delicate, firm flesh. When you buy them, make sure that the shells are tightly closed. Your fishmonger will be happy to open the shells and remove the meat, but in any event you must rinse the shellfish thoroughly again before preparing them. Instead of skewers, our chef uses sprigs of rosemary, the firm leaves of which give the seafood a special flavor.

In order to unite the flavors of the sea with those of the land, Francesca de Giovannini has opted to use porcini mushrooms, which are extremely popular in Italy. They are easily recognizable from their compact base and round, convex cap. As a final touch, the kebabs are wrapped in fatty bacon – a culinary treat!

The creamed cornmeal, often eaten in the Veneto region, the home of polenta, gives this dish its somewhat rustic character. Corn was introduced to Italy from Mexico in the 16th century and in the north it soon replaced staples such as fava beans, garbanzo beans, and bread. This cereal is grown mainly in northern Italy and even today remains an essential part of the regional cuisine.

Chives, which are chopped finely and added to the polenta in this dish, have a slightly peppery taste. With their bright green color they can be used to good effect as a substitute for onions.

For the cornmeal cream, bring 2 cups/ 500 ml water to the boil with a good pinch of coarse salt. Trickle in the cornmeal slowly and cook for 40 minutes, stirring constantly.

Chop the chives very finely and add to the cornmeal porridge. Stir and set aside.

Cut the rosemary sprigs diagonally at the lower ends and remove all the leaves except for a few at the top. Cut the porcini into large, even-sized cubes.

alla Francesca

Thread 3 Venus clams and 2 mushroom cubes onto each rosemary sprig.

Wrap each kebab completely in fatty bacon.

Place the kebabs in an ovenproof dish and season with salt and pepper. Pour over the vegetable oil and cook for 2–3 minutes at 400° F/200° C. Pour in the white wine and bake for another 3 minutes. Serve each kebab on a bed of polenta and garnish with rosemary.

Monkfish

Preparation time:	*40 minutes*	
Cooking time:	*1 hour 5 minutes*	
Difficulty:	*	

Serves 4

2¼ lb/1 kg	monkfish
8 oz/200 g	pancetta (or other slab bacon)
	salt
	white pepper
8 oz/200 g	potatoes
⅞ stick/	
100 g	butter
2 cups/500 ml	milk
2 tbsp	olive oil
3½ tbsp/50 g	olive purée (*tapenade*)

For the fish stock:

1	carrot
1	onion
1	tomato
3 sprigs	parsley
1 stick	celery
3 cloves	garlic
	head and large bones of the monkfish
	salt
	pepper

For the garnish:

	black olives (optional)
	parsley

The Adriatic coast in the Marche region has fish in abundance and meets ten percent of the demand for fish in Italy. Every day, fishing boats dock in the main ports all along the coast, laden with sardines, octopus, turbot, monkfish, and other fish in their catch.

The Adriatic monkfish dish "cartoceto" unites produce from the sea and the land. This traditional dish, which is easy to prepare, provides additional proof of how delicious Italian cuisine can be: These fish fillets wrapped in bacon are an absolute delight.

Monkfish live on the sandy or clay seabed off the coast. Their fine, succulent flesh, sometimes reminiscent of lobster, is suitable for a wide variety of piquant dishes. If monkfish is unavailable, you can substitute cod.

Pancetta, on the other hand, is an indispensable ingredient in this recipe. This smoked, fatty Italian bacon is still made by the butchers themselves. The meat is separated from the skin of the pig and then spiced with nutmeg, cloves, juniper, and cinnamon, for a slightly sweet taste.

Alberto Melagrana cooks the monkfish with a black *tapenade*, which is diluted with fish stock to make a sauce. This piquant-flavored paste, which is used a great deal in southern France, is made from olives, sometimes with the addition of anchovies, garlic, and thyme. *Tapenade* goes well with meat, fish, and toasted bread. There are olives galore in the Marche region: Ascoli Piceno is famous for its stuffed olives, while the province of Cartoceto is known for its top-class olive oil. The chef sometimes substitutes a truffle sauce for the *tapenade* and maintains that this alone transforms the monkfish into a culinary delight.

Skin the monkfish. Run a knife along the backbone and separate the fillets. Set aside the head and the large bones.

For the fish stock, place the peeled and diced carrot, onion, tomato, parsley, celery, peeled cloves of garlic, and the head and large bones of the monkfish in a large saucepan of water. Simmer for about 1 hour. Season with salt and pepper, then set aside.

Spread a double layer of plastic wrap on the work surface and lay the slices of pancetta on this. Then lay the monkfish fillets on the bacon and sprinkle with salt and pepper. Roll the fish in the bacon with the aid of the plastic wrap, then carefully remove the wrap.

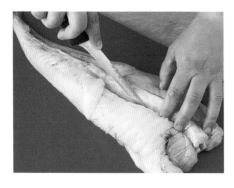

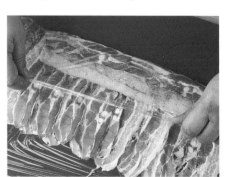

"Cartoceto"

Peel the potatoes and cut into small pieces. Cook for 20 minutes in boiling water. Pass through a strainer with the butter. Stir in the milk and season with salt and pepper.

Fry the monkfish roll in olive oil in a skillet until it is golden yellow, then transfer to the oven and bake for about 3 minutes at 340° F/170° C. Cut the roll into medallions.

Strain the fish stock. Heat 1 scant cup/ 200 ml stock and stir in the tapenade. Arrange the potato purée and monkfish medallions on plates and pour over the tapenade sauce. Garnish with olives, if desired, and parsley.

Dried Cod

Preparation time: 25 minutes
Desalting the fish: 48 hours
Cooking time: 30 minutes
Difficulty: ★

Serves 4

1¼ lb/500 g	dried cod (stockfish)
4 oz/100 g	potatoes
1	onion

1 stick	celery
8 oz/200 g	tomatoes
4 tbsp	olive oil
	salt
	pepper

The Fischettis are a good example of a typical, close-knit, southern Italian family.

The family's restaurant, "L'Oasis," is poised like a beehive high up in Vallesaccarda in the countryside around Avellino. On their magnificent estate, the 13 members of the Fischetti clan welcome their guests and experiment with traditional regional recipes, creating variations on them as a labor of love.

Dried cod is very popular, especially in the area around Naples. It can be prepared in many different ways. In bygone times, dried cod was important for a very specific reason: Salting and drying was the only method of preserving fish. With abundant supplies ensured, the population was even able to survive famines.

This colorful dish devised by the Fischetti family is typical of the Mediterranean. It owes its characteristic flavor to celery leaves; this plant is in plentiful supply in autumn and winter and is particularly appetizing when added to soups, sauces, and goulash.

The tomatoes add a classic Neapolitan accent to this dish. In Italy, tomatoes are eaten almost daily. The tomato, a member of the solanum family, used to be grown in gardens for home consumption, but now tomatoes are cultivated on a grand scale, especially in southern Italy, and are exported all over the world.

This dried-cod recipe from the Fischetti family is simple to prepare, yet highly sophisticated!

Using a large knife, cut the dried cod into even-sized pieces and remove the bones.

Place the pieces of fish in a salad bowl full of water for 48 hours to remove the salt, changing the water several times.

Peel and chop the potatoes and onion. Wash the celery and cut the leaves into small pieces. Blanch, skin, and dice all the tomatoes.

"Casa Fischetti"

Heat the olive oil in a pan and sauté the onion for 5 minutes. Add the potatoes and cook for a further 5 minutes. Add the tomatoes and season with salt and pepper. Cook for another 5 minutes, stirring several times with a wooden spatula.

Drain the dried cod and remove the remaining bones. Add the pieces of fish to the vegetables in the pan and simmer for about 5 minutes.

Add the chopped celery leaves. Simmer for 10 minutes, stirring, then transfer the cod and vegetables onto plates to serve.

Mussels in

Preparation time: 40 minutes
Cooking time: 50 minutes
Difficulty: ★

Serves 4

4½ lb/2 kg	mussels
1	onion
1 scant cup/ 200 ml	white wine
1 scant cup/ 200 ml	light cream
2 tsp/10 g	butter
1 bunch	marjoram
	salt
	pepper

For the salad:

2	red bell peppers
2 tbsp	olive oil

	coarse salt
2	eggplants
2	large onions
	sunflower oil for frying
1–1¼ cups / 125–150 g	capers
scant ½ cup/ 100 ml	white wine
scant ½ cup/ 100 ml	balsamic vinegar
	salt and pepper to taste

For the garnish:

	marjoram

This sophisticated hot appetizer is one of Sergio Pais' creations. The creamed mussels are served with a salad that tastes of sunshine and the south. This colorful dish is easy to prepare and will delight your guests. The Gulf of Taranto, which lies between the "heel" and "sole" of the boot of Italy, is famous for its mussel beds. The inhabitants call it *Mar piccolo*, or "little sea." The clear waters of the gulf are ideal for the cultivation of mussels.

When buying, choose only tightly closed mussels. They should be eaten within three days of harvesting. If any of them have broken shells or are slightly open, throw them away. The beards must be removed from the mussels and any seaweed removed from the shells. They should then be brushed thoroughly under running water.

The marjoram sauce is excellent and quite outstanding with the mussels. Marjoram is often used in cooking in the Mediterranean. Originally from Asia, it is a relative of oregano but has a milder, subtler flavor with a taste reminiscent of mint and basil. It is used to flavor tomato dishes, salad dressings, stuffings, fish, and soups.

The salad consists of eggplants, onions, red pepper, and capers, and is enhanced with a dash of olive oil. Balsamic vinegar is made by reducing grape must, just as it was 900 years ago by the Duke d'Este and other noblemen in the area around Modena. Although regarded as a medicinal product, it was presented as a gift among the higher social echelons. High-quality balsamic vinegar is very expensive and, for this reason, is used very sparingly.

Lay the bell peppers on a baking sheet, pour over the olive oil, and sprinkle with salt. Roast in the oven for about 45 minutes, then remove the skin and seeds and cut into thin strips. Dice the eggplants and peel and slice the onions.

Pour the sunflower oil into a pan and sauté the eggplant cubes. Remove from the pan and drain. Brown the onions in another pan.

Transfer the eggplants, onions, and bell pepper strips to a salad bowl and add the capers.

Marjoram Sauce

Pour the white wine and balsamic vinegar into a small pan and reduce by half. Pour the reduced liquid onto the salad and stir carefully, then add salt and pepper.

Clean the mussels and remove the beards. Chop the onion. Heat the onion in a saucepan with the white wine. Add the mussels, cover, and infuse for 10 minutes. Remove the meat from the mussel shells.

Stir the cream, butter, and marjoram leaves together over a low heat. Season with salt and pepper and mix thoroughly. Add the mussel meat. Simmer for 3–4 minutes. Serve the salad with the mussels and sauce and garnish with a few marjoram leaves.

Red Mullet Rolls

Preparation time: 30 minutes
Cooking time: 20 minutes
Difficulty: ★★

Serves 4

1½ lb/600 g	red mullet
4 oz/100 g	leeks
	olive oil
4 oz/100 g	salted pancetta (or other slab bacon)

10 oz/250 g	peeled chestnuts
scant ½ cup/ 100 ml	white wine
1 clove	garlic
	salt
	pepper

For this recipe, Alfonso Caputo drew inspiration from a traditional Neapolitan dish of small pork roulades known in the Neapolitan dialect as *braciola*. Alfonso stuffs his red mullet rolls with pancetta and serves them with chestnuts in white wine and deep-fried leek. If you are unable to obtain red mullet, use red snapper instead.

Tasty fish such as red mullet, gold bream, sea perch, and anchovies are caught in the Gulf of Naples and the neighboring Gulf of Salerno, and arrive on the fishmongers' stalls fresh from the boats. When you fillet the red mullet, try not to remove the skin – it is very thin and almost impossible to detach – but always remove the numerous bones in pairs. You can tell where any bones remain by stroking your finger towards the tail. The fish fillets are covered in pancetta and then rolled up. Pancetta is lean bacon made from pork belly and is available salted, smoked, dried, or spiced with pepper, nutmeg, cloves,

juniper berries, or cinnamon. It is usually available in slabs or rolled.

The leek is chopped very finely and deep-fried, and is used as a garnish. You will also need a little more leek to tie up the rolls, or alternatively they can be secured with wooden cocktail sticks.

Chestnuts are often served as an accompaniment to meat. Sweet chestnut trees grow in large numbers on the wooded slopes around Naples, and Sergio Pais is particularly fond of those from the Serino area. He recommends serving two rolls with chestnuts and a little leek per person. The combination of red mullet and leek is unusual, even in Italian cuisine – but definitely worth a try.

Cut open the red mullet along the underside. Cut across the tail end and divide the backbone. Detach the fillets by running the knife the length of the backbone.

Cut the leeks into thin strips. Deep-fry in a pan of olive oil for 5 minutes. Drain on paper towels.

Cut the pancetta into thin slices. Lay a slice on each fillet and roll together.

with Chestnuts

Tie up the rolls with a narrow strip of green leek.

Heat the chestnuts in some oil in a pan. Pour in the white wine and simmer for 10 minutes.

Add the red mullet rolls with the finely sliced garlic to the pan. Season with salt and pepper. Cover and cook for 4–5 minutes. Place two red mullet rolls with a few chestnuts on each plate and garnish with the deep-fried leek.

Sardines

Preparation time: 30 minutes
Soaking time: 1 hour
Marinating: 12–48 hours
Cooking time: 30 minutes
Difficulty: ★

Serves 4

⅓ cup/50 g	raisins
1½ lb/600 g	sardines
1 scant cup/ 100 g	flour

1⅔ cups/ 400 ml	extra-virgin olive oil
12 oz/300 g	onions
scant ½ cup/ 50 g	pine nuts
scant ½ cup/ 100 ml	red wine vinegar
	salt

For centuries, the natives of the Veneto region have been enjoying sardines – known as *sarde in saor* in the local dialect – cooked in the same way that Biancarosa Zecchin prepares them. They are first coated in flour, then fried in oil, and finally marinated in a mixture of vinegar and onions. The nobility in the Veneto region used to enhance the dish with raisins and pine nuts to distinguish themselves from ordinary folk, who could not afford these ingredients. The dried fruit makes the dish more nutritious and gives it a festive touch. Sardines *in saor* are served in restaurants in Venice both as a small appetizer and as a main course.

In those parts of the lagoons around Venice where there are less *vaporetti* and motor-boat traffic, sardines are still plentiful. They used to constitute the majority of the day's catch, and were affordable by ordinary families as well as by the more affluent.

Medium-sized and smaller sardines are perfect for this recipe. When preparing these small fish, just remove the head and nothing else. After you have dipped them in flour, tap them with your finger to remove any excess. The oil used for frying the sardines is then used to sauté the chopped onion.

Biancarosa Zecchin recommends marinating the sardines for at least 12 hours before eating them. If they are marinated for as long as 48 hours, they will develop an even stronger flavor.

Serve three or four sardines per person. Spread the onion mixture on top and sprinkle with raisins and pine nuts, if desired.

Soak the raisins for 1 hour in lukewarm water. Remove the fish heads, then cut open and gut the sardines. Rinse them thoroughly under running water and pat them dry carefully.

Coat the sardines in flour.

Heat the olive oil in a large skillet. Fry the sardines for 5 minutes on each side. When they are golden yellow, drain them on paper towels. Reserve the oil.

in Saor

Peel and slice the onions.

Sauté the onions for 5 minutes in the oil used for frying the sardines. Stir frequently to ensure they cook evenly. Add the pine nuts, drained raisins, vinegar, and salt to taste. Cook for 15 minutes.

Arrange the sardines on a plate and spread the onion mixture on top. Leave to absorb the flavors for at least 12 hours. Serve cold, with a little strained marinade.

Sole

Preparation time: 15 minutes
Cooking time: 15 minutes
Difficulty: ★

Serves 4

4	sole, each 8 oz/200 g
1 clove	garlic
½ bunch	parsley
½	lemon
4 tbsp	olive oil

	salt
20	black olives

For the garnish:

lemon wedges

In the small port of Giulianova in Abruzzi, Maddalena Beccaceci, affectionately known as "Nena," is renowned as an imaginative chef. Time and again, she cooks dishes in her restaurant that are quite extraordinary.

Rooted firmly in the traditional cuisine of her native region, she presents here a dish that is quite typical of the town where she was born. Sole à la Nena is a minimalist recipe and very easy to prepare. With only a few ingredients, Nena transforms ordinary fillets of sole into a real culinary delight.

Sole, with their near-perfect oval form, should be at least 8 inches/21 centimeters long before sold. They weigh between 8 ounces/200 grams and 2¼ pounds/ 1 kilogram.

The ancient Romans were admirers of this fish, which they ate marinated, steamed, or in soup. The delicate, practically boneless flesh needs only brief cooking. If you have difficulty gutting the fish, just ask your fishmonger to do it for you. You can also prepare this dish using monkfish or sea pike.

Sole à la Nena would not be the same without parsley. Indeed, without this aromatic plant, Italian and southern European cuisine as a whole would be much the poorer. Parsley is available all year round and should be fresh and bright green in color.

In Mediterranean cookery, black olives are used mainly as flavorings. Olives are preserved either in oil or brine. They enhance many dishes, but are used also in bread making and for garnishes. Greek and Italian olives are considered the best in the world.

Use a knife to remove the scales and gut the fish. Cut off the edges of the fish with kitchen scissors.

Cut into the sole behind the gills. Hold the skin between your thumb and index finger and carefully loosen a section. Then hold the loosened skin with a cloth and pull to remove it, working from the head toward the tail fin.

Peel and chop the garlic. Wash the parsley and chop finely. Squeeze the lemon.

à la Nena

Lay the sole in a large, ovenproof dish or a fish kettle.

Put the garlic, lemon juice, and parsley in a small dish. Add the olive oil and salt to taste, then stir to combine. Pour the mixture over the sole and add 4–5 tbsp/ 60–75 ml water.

Cover with aluminum foil and cook in the oven for 10–15 minutes. Add the black olives. Transfer to plates and garnish with lemon wedges.

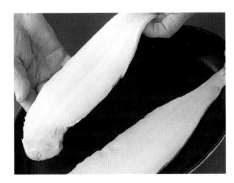

Salmon Trout

Preparation time:	*35 minutes*
Cooking time:	*10 minutes*
Difficulty:	★★

Serves 4

2	salmon trout, each 1 lb 6 oz/600 g
⅓ cup/50 g	wheat flour
	salt
scant ½ stick/ 50 g	butter
scant ½ cup/ 100 ml	white wine
1	unwaxed orange

For the fish stock:

	1 carrot
	1 onion

3	tomatoes
1 stick	celery
	trout heads, bones and fins
3	basil leaves
	salt to taste

For the garnish:

1	orange
1	tomato
	chervil

For centuries, the major rivers draining the water from the Apennine Mountains and The Alps contained trout, perch, carp, sturgeon, and Allis shad (alosa alosa) in abundance. Industrial development and also, of course, environmental pollution have put an end to this plentiful supply of fish, and today most trout are farmed.

Although stocks of salmon trout have declined dramatically, some still remain in River Serchio, near Sauro Brunicardi's restaurant in Ponte a Moriano. They were customarily broiled or fried; here, however, our chef serves them in an orange sauce.

Sauro Brunicardi uses trout weighing 1 pound 6 ounces/600 grams each. If you use larger fish, the fillets will need dividing. After filleting the fish, carefully remove all the bones with tweezers.

It is of course easier to ask your fishmonger to fillet the fish for you, but ask him to save the heads, bones, and fins for the fish stock. You will also need celery, onions, carrots, and basil for the fish stock. Tomatoes can also be added if desired.

First, Sauro Brunicardi fries the fish – with the skin on – in a coating of flour. The skin side should be fried first; this holds the fish together while it is cooking and the fat makes the fillets brown and crisp on the outside. Then turn the fish and fry on the other side.

This recipe is also excellent for trout, swordfish, or turbot – the flavor of all these fish will develop fully in the orange sauce.

Cut the trout along the underside and gut them. Cut along the backbone and then cut horizontally just above the tail. Remove the fillets and reserve the heads, bones, and fins for the fish stock.

For the fish stock, peel the carrot and cut into pieces. Peel and quarter the onion and quarter the tomatoes. Cut the celery into small sticks.

Add the heads, bones, and fins of the trout with the vegetables, basil, and salt to a saucepan of boiling water. Leave to infuse for 1 hour over a low heat, then strain and set aside.

with Orange Sauce

Place the flour on a plate with a little salt. Turn the fish fillets in the flour to coat them, first the flesh side, then the skin side. Tap with your finger to remove any excess flour.

Melt the butter in a large skillet. When it is hot, transfer the fish fillets to the skillet, skin side down. Turn and cook for about 6 minutes until golden brown. Pour off the fat.

Pour the white wine into the pan. Add the juice from the orange, the orange peel cut into strips, and the strained fish stock. Reduce for 5 minutes over a high heat. Transfer the fillets to plates and pour over the sauce. Garnish with small pieces of orange, orange slices, tomato, and chervil.

Meat & Poultry

Lamb

Preparation time:	25 minutes
Cooking time:	30 minutes
Difficulty:	✫

Serves 4

3¼ lb/1.5 kg	leg of lamb
4 tbsp	olive oil
1 clove	garlic
	salt
1 sprig	rosemary
2	peppercorns

4 tbsp	white wine
1	lemon
2	eggs
1 tsp/5 g	grated parmesan

For the garnish:

	rosemary
	cherry tomatoes

There are many typical regional meat dishes in Abruzzi, including this lamb dish, which is particularly popular at Christmas and Easter.

Maddalena Beccaceci's Abruzzi-style lamb has a pronounced rustic character. Today, shepherds still drive their flocks of sheep up to the Alpine pastures when the warm weather begins. On the high plains, the animals live entirely on fresh grass and herbs, which is why the meat is supremely tasty and so sought-after all over Italy. Shoulder of lamb is just as good as leg of lamb in this recipe.

The rural population in Abruzzi once lived mainly on eggs and cheese, so this festive dish naturally contains both these ingredients.

Parmesan, which is still made by hand, is the king of Italian cheeses. It was probably first produced in Tuscany in the 11th century, and a certain Bartolomeo Riva was apparently responsible for introducing the first *parmigiano reggiano* to the people in 1612. Today, parmesan can only be produced in the provinces of Parma, Reggio Emilia, Modena, Mantua, and Bologna. It is made from cow's milk from which some of the cream has been removed. It is called *vecchio*, meaning "old," after maturing for one year. The designation *stravecchio*, "extremely old," can only be used after the parmesan has matured for three years.

Rosemary is indispensable in this recipe. This typically Mediterranean herb has a mild, piquant taste and its fragrance evokes the sun-drenched countryside. Both the fresh and dried leaves of this evergreen shrub are used for flavoring, but they must be used sparingly.

Cut the lamb into cubes. Heat the olive oil and the chopped clove of garlic in a pan and add the meat. Season with salt, then brown the meat all over. Add the chopped rosemary leaves and crushed peppercorns. Braise the mixture for about 10 minutes.

Pour in the white wine and boil for 10 minutes to reduce.

Squeeze the lemon and pour the juice into a bowl. Add the eggs and parmesan and season with salt.

Abruzzi Style

Beat the lemon juice, eggs, and cheese thoroughly with a fork.

Pour the mixture carefully over the meat.

Shake the pan and stir with a wooden spoon until the eggs are set. Serve the meat garnished with the rosemary and cherry tomatoes.

Lamb Cutlets

Preparation time: 25 minutes
Cooking time: 15 minutes
Difficulty: ★

Serves 4

1½ lb/600 g	loin of lamb
4 tbsp	white wine
	coarse salt
½ bunch	flat-leaved parsley
2	onions

3 sprigs	rosemary
4 oz/100 g	dried mild chile
5 tbsp	olive oil
	salt
	pepper

There is more to Campagna, a landscape of contrasts, than Naples or Pompeii. Visitors to the countryside are surprised to find tracts of land of great beauty. As far as traditional cuisine is concerned, too, there is a great deal to discover in Campagna. The small town of Irpinia lies in the province of Avellino and is famous throughout Italy for its filberts. In addition, it has an extraordinary culinary heritage, handed down by the shepherds of Abruzzi.

The piquant, aromatic lamb cutlets presented here by Michelina Fischetti used to be served on festive occasions. In this recipe, our chef uses only local produce, reflecting the motto of the natives of Irpinia who are very attached to their birthplace and would never leave it voluntarily. The lamb is "washed" in white wine to remove any excess fat and thus make the dish more digestible. Depending on availability, you can substitute a young kid, a very popular delicacy in Calabria, for the lamb.

Chiles, called *peperoncini* in Italian, should be used sparingly, but they are absolutely crucial for the authentic flavor of this dish. Chiles are available in many shapes and colors on Italian markets. To make them slightly less hot, remove the seeds and the whitish skin inside. Chiles dry well, and will then keep for at least a year. Rosemary is also indispensable in this recipe. This aromatic plant grows everywhere in the Mediterranean region and, with its slightly piquant flavor, is excellent for marinades. Parsley also has a strong flavor: flat-leaved parsley more so than the curly-leaved variety. It is available all year round and should be bright green with crisp, firm leaves and stalks.

Using a large knife, cut the loin of lamb into individual cutlets.

Lay the cutlets in a dish and pour over the wine and a little water. Add a good pinch of coarse salt and mix together with your hands.

Wash and finely chop the parsley. Peel the onions and cut into small pieces. Remove the rosemary leaves from the stalks and finely chop the chile.

"Irpinia"

Heat the olive oil and sauté the onions. Add the chopped chile and sauté for another 3 minutes.

Add the cutlets and the wine mixture to the pan. Season with salt and pepper. Brown for 3 minutes.

Pour in a scant ½ cup/100 ml water and simmer for 5 minutes. Add the rosemary and sprinkle with chopped parsley. Serve the lamb cutlets "Irpinia" on plates with the sauce.

Veal Cutlets

Preparation time:	45 minutes
Cooking time:	15 minutes
Difficulty:	★

Serves 4

1½ lb/600 g	veal fillet
6 oz/150 g	Parma ham
12	sage leaves
1¼ lb/500 g	broccoli
	coarse salt
2	zucchini

1 cup/250 ml	milk
1 scant cup/	
100 g	flour
	olive oil for deep frying
1 tbsp	sunflower oil
1 scant cup/	
200 ml	white wine
1 cup/250 ml	meat stock
1½ tbsp/20 g	butter
	salt
	pepper

These veal cutlets with sage have a real flavor of Italy, and are simply delicious. They are prepared for festive occasions, especially in Lazio.

Knuckle, shoulder, or leg cutlets are easily recognizable by their regular, oval form. In Italy, *scaloppine* are normally cut from the fillet. They are hammered with a meat mallet, which is sometimes notched on one side, and are suitable for frying or braising. The favorite way of cooking them in Milan is with a coating of breadcrumbs.

For this nutritious dish, Sergio Pais must have Parma ham, made from the leg of the pig. In Tuscany, it is flavored with garlic, cloves, and pepper and, after being preserved in this way for four weeks, has to be kept for a long time to mature. After six months, the part not covered by skin is spread with pig fat, and the ham is then left to mature for another six months, during which time it is carefully observed. The crown of the Duchy of Parma is stamped on the skin of every ham as illustrious proof of its origin.

The slightly piquant taste of sage, which is frequently used in Italian cuisine, gives this dish its characteristic flavor. Sage grows in temperate zones and, although it is mainly used to flavor meat, it is also used for bean and pasta dishes.

Broccoli comes from southern Italy and is cultivated mainly in Apulia. This brassica is rich in vitamins and minerals and is in season from April to October. Its name comes from the Greek *brotrytis*, the approximate meaning of which is "to form a grape." The broccoli florets should be firm and dense and the stalk should be very firm. Broccoli needs to be cooked for 10–15 minutes.

Cut the veal fillet into even-sized pieces and hammer into cutlets.

Cut the Parma ham to the same length as the cutlets. Lay the meat on a work surface. Place a slice of ham and a sage leaf on each cutlet and secure with a wooden cocktail stick.

Remove the broccoli florets from the stalk. Simmer the florets for about 10 minutes in a pan of water with a good pinch of coarse salt. Drain, and cool in ice water.

with Sage

Cut the zucchini into small sticks. Dip in milk, then roll in flour to coat. Deep-fry in olive oil, then drain.

Heat the sunflower oil in a pan and fry the cutlets for about 3 minutes. Remove the wooden cocktail sticks and quench the cutlets with the white wine. Add the meat stock and cook for another 3 minutes.

Add the butter. Shake the pan back and forth. Season with salt and pepper. Serve the cutlets on plates with the deep-fried zucchini sticks, broccoli, and sauce.

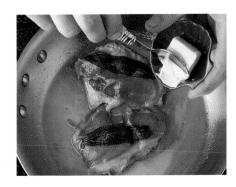

Loin of Suckling

Preparation time: 25 minutes
Cooking time: 55 minutes
Difficulty: ★

Serves 4

4 tbsp	extra-virgin olive oil
2¼ lb/1 kg	loin of suckling pig
	salt
1 tbsp	bouquet garni herbs
1 scant cup/ 50 g	breadcrumbs

For the garlic sauce:

5 cloves	garlic
	salt
2 cups/500 ml	light cream
1 tbsp	cornstarch

For this recipe, Sauro Brunicardi has drawn inspiration from a traditional Tuscan dish of roast pork with herbs (*arista di maiale*). The chef has additionally enhanced the pork by coating the edge of each piece of meat with a thick garlic and herb sauce and sprinkling it with a mixture of breadcrumbs and bouquet garni herbs known in Italian as *pan alle herbe*.

Suckling pig has been regarded as a delicacy since the Middle Ages. The piglet is slaughtered before it reaches two months of age and should then weigh at least 33 pounds/ 15 kilograms. The meat is white, tender, and tasty. For this recipe, choose a loin consisting of 4–5 loin chops; these are not divided until they have been cooked in the oven. A loin of lamb can be prepared in exactly the same way.

For frying the meat, Sauro Brunicardi prefers to use extra-virgin olive oil originating from Lucca. This oil has a wonderfully luminous, green-yellow color and has the taste and smell of green apples.

The loin chops with their coating of garlic and herb sauce are wrapped in aluminum foil, before being cooked in the oven for the second time in such a way that only the edge with the sauce is exposed. This results in a deliciously fragrant, crisp crust.

As an accompaniment, Sauro Brunicardi recommends braised vegetables: for instance, a medley of spinach, broccoli, and cauliflower with potatoes, to add a touch of color. You can also serve poached vegetables with it, if you prefer. Serve the loin chops with carrots, zucchini, potatoes, and the garlic and herb sauce, and decorate the plates with a drizzle of sauce from the meat juices.

Remove the outer, papery covering of the garlic cloves. Using a small knife, cut off both ends and remove the skin, as well as any green shoots.

Put the garlic cloves and salt to taste in a saucepan with the cream. Bring to the boil and simmer for 5 minutes, then mix in a blender.

Return the blended sauce to the saucepan. Mix the cornstarch with a little of the sauce, add to the contents of the pan, and continue to stir for 5 minutes until the sauce is smooth and thick.

Pig with Herbs

Pour the olive oil into an ovenproof dish. Place the meat in the dish and season with salt. Bake in the oven for 40 minutes at 430° F/220° C.

Transfer the meat to a chopping board and separate the cutlets. Mix the bouquet garni herbs and the breadcrumbs.

Spread garlic cream over the fatty edge of the cutlets and sprinkle with the herb mixture. Wrap the cutlets in aluminum foil so that only the coated edge is showing. Return to the oven for a further 5 minutes before serving.

Pork Fillet

Preparation time:	40 minutes
Cooling time:	30 minutes
Cooking time:	15 minutes
Difficulty:	★

Serves 4

1½ lb/600 g	pork fillets
1 tsp	flour
3 tbsp	olive oil
2¼ lb/1 kg	broccoli
	salt
3 cloves	garlic

Dough for crust:

12 oz/300 g	sliced bread
1½ tbsp/20 g	butter

2	egg whites
3 stalks	parsley
2 tsp/10 g	chopped thyme
2 tsp/10 g	chopped marjoram
2 tsp/10 g	chopped rosemary
2 tsp/10 g	chopped savory
1	bay leaf
	salt and pepper to taste

For the basil sauce (optional):

½ bunch	basil
5 stalks	parsley
4 tbsp	olive oil

The inhabitants of the Marche region are justifiably proud of their area. The countryside with its medieval towns and centuries-old oak forests is rich in history and a popular tourist destination.

The cuisine of the Marche region also has much to offer. The aromatic herbs that grow there in abundance are excellent with meat, fish, or vegetables.

This traditional dish of pork fillet with a herb crust is a fine example of the sophistication of the regional cuisine. It is easy to prepare and a classic dish for Sunday lunch.

Pork is the Italians' favorite meat and they are consequently very demanding as far as its quality is concerned. According to our chef, extremely tender meat is obtained from the livestock in the Marche region that are for the most part raised in free-range conditions. Alberto Melagrana rolls the pork fillet in a herb-flavored dough before putting it in the oven.

Wild marjoram, known in the dialect as *persichina*, is typical of the region. It tastes and smells like a mixture of mint and basil. Marjoram has a milder taste than its close relative, oregano.

To enhance the pork, Alberto Melagrana suggests serving a truffle sauce, provided fresh truffles are available. If you opt for this, be sparing with the other flavorings. Cauliflower can also be substituted for broccoli.

For the dough, combine the bread, butter, egg whites, parsley, thyme, marjoram, rosemary, savory, and bay leaf with salt and pepper in a blender. Leave the dough to stand in a cool place for 30 minutes.

Dust the pork fillets lightly with flour. Fry in 1 tbsp olive oil until nearly cooked. Leave to cool.

Roll out the dough thinly. Using plastic wrap, roll the fillets in the dough. Remove the wrap and bake the rolled fillets in the oven at 340° F/170° C for about 6 minutes.

with a Herb Crust

Remove the broccoli florets from the stalk. Simmer the florets for about 5 minutes in salted water. Drain, and cool in ice water.

Heat the unpeeled garlic cloves with the remaining olive oil in a pan. Add the broccoli florets and sauté.

Cut the rolled pork fillets into medallions. Prepare the basil sauce, if using. Serve the fillets in their herb crust with the broccoli, using the basil sauce as garnish.

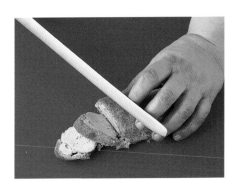

Rabbit

Preparation time:	25 minutes
Soaking time:	30 minutes
Cooking time:	1 hour
Difficulty:	★

Serves 4

1 good pinch	saffron threads
1	rabbit weighing 2 lb 3 oz/1 kg
3 cloves	garlic
4 tbsp	olive oil
1 sprig	thyme

2	sage leaves
2	black peppercorns
	salt
4 tbsp	white wine

When October arrives, Navelli, in the province of L'Aquila, becomes a hive of activity. Seasonal workers from all over Italy descend on the Abruzzi region in fall when the harvesting of saffron, the most expensive spice in the world, begins. A large number of men and women are employed to complete the harvest within two weeks, and to remove the precious stigmas (threads) from the blossoms by hand. Saffron from L'Aquila is internationally renowned and the Italians obviously enjoy cooking with this fine spice too.

Maddalena Beccaceci flavors her rabbit dish with saffron from Navelli. This traditional dish is easy to prepare and an unforgettable culinary experience.

Rabbit is highly regarded in Italy because of its firm, very tasty flesh. Rabbits should have a well-rounded back and a pale liver without any spots. When preparing the dish, be careful that the meat does not dry out, as this can easily happen. It is also possible to use a chicken instead of the rabbit in this recipe.

This rabbit dish would not be the same without fresh herbs. In particular, Mediterranean cuisine is scarcely imaginable without thyme, a member of the labiate family. Sage is used for the widest possible range of specialties in Italy; with its strong, slightly bitter flavor, it is used for sausages and other meat dishes. This plant, which grows in temperate zones, has been treasured since time immemorial for its healing powers – not least because it makes rich food more easily digestible.

This wonderful rabbit with saffron recipe is an exquisite dish for a festive meal.

Place the saffron threads in a small bowl and pour over 4 tbsp warm water. Soak for 30 minutes.

Divide the rabbit in two and carefully cut into joints.

Peel the garlic and fry in the olive oil. Add the thyme, sage, and peppercorns.

with Saffron

Add the rabbit joints to the skillet. Turn several times, to cover in oil and herbs. Season with salt and then fry for about 30 minutes.

Pour in the white wine and stir with a wooden spoon. Reduce the liquid for about 15 minutes.

Add the saffron. Simmer for another 5 minutes. Serve the rabbit portions on plates with some of the sauce.

Ossobuco

Preparation time: 30 minutes
Cooking time: 1 hour 50 minutes
Difficulty: ☆

Serves 4

4 slices	leg of veal
1 scant cup/ 100 g	flour
3 tbsp	sunflower oil
½ cup/120 ml	white wine
2	unwaxed lemons
2	anchovy fillets
scant ½ stick/ 50 g	butter
	salt

	pepper
1 bunch	parsley

For the saffron risotto:

1	small onion
3 tbsp	olive oil
1 cup/200 g	Arborio rice
3 cups/750 ml	chicken stock
½ tsp/3 g	saffron powder
	salt
	pepper
4½ oz/125 g	grated parmesan
¾ stick/90 g	butter

For the garnish:

	saffron threads

Ossobuco alla Milanese is a classic in the cuisine of Lombardy and is eaten on the widest variety of occasions in northern Italy. Literally translated, the name means "bone with a hole," and refers to the slices of veal knuckle. They are cooked for a long time in white wine, which makes them extremely tasty. The chef has introduced a personal note into this recipe, adding anchovy fillets and lemon peel to the list of ingredients.

Veal knuckle, a favorite with gourmets, is found between the foot and shoulder of the calf. Only buy veal of the best quality that is reddish pink in color. Ask your butcher to cut slices from the leg of veal that are about 1 inch/2.5 centimeters thick.

Rice is so important in the cuisine of Lombardy that meat – in contrast with the rest of Italy – is pushed into second place. There are about 8,000 known varieties of rice, distinguished by the type of grain – short, long, or medium.

Rice, which originally grew on dry, sandy soil, was being cultivated in China in 3,000 B.C. Arabian travelers are supposed to have brought it back with them to Europe, where it was first cultivated in Sicily. It was only in the 19th century that rice began to be grown on a grand scale in Italy, on the Po plain. In Milan, saffron risotto is also called *risotto giallo*, "yellow risotto." This specialty, featuring generous quantities of butter and parmesan, is now justifiably internationally famous.

Saffron, which has been cultivated in Abruzzi for many years, is obtained from the flower of a species of purple crocus. In the 13th century, according to historical anecdote, Pope Celestin IV revered saffron above all else and, despite its high cost, the Milanese are supposed to have perfumed his bathwater with it.

Coat the slices of leg of veal in flour and fry for 10 minutes in sunflower oil.

Pour in the white wine and simmer everything for about 1 hour 30 minutes. Remove the zest from the lemons and squeeze them.

For the risotto, peel and chop the onion. Sauté in olive oil. Add the rice and cook slowly for 2 minutes until it is transparent, then gradually pour in the chicken stock. Simmer for about 16 minutes.

alla Milanese

Stir in the saffron, season with salt and pepper, and infuse for 2 minutes.

Add the parmesan cheese and butter, and stir.

Add strips of lemon zest to the meat and pour in the lemon juice. Add the anchovy fillets and butter, then season with salt and pepper. Simmer for 10 minutes. Sprinkle with chopped parsley and place the meat on the risotto to serve. Garnish with saffron threads.

Duck

Preparation time: 30 minutes
Cooking time: 2 hours 10 minutes
Difficulty: ✶✶

Serves 4

1	small oven-ready duck
3	pears
1	lemon
4 oz/100 g	white grapes
4 oz/100 g	red grapes
1 tbsp	extra-virgin olive oil

1 scant cup/200 ml	dry white wine
12	cherries
⅜ stick/40 g	butter
2 tbsp	sugar

This duck, surrounded by an abundance of fruit, could almost be a still life by one of the Old Masters. In fact, Biancarosa Zecchin has taken a 17th-century recipe and adapted it to modern tastes. Her husband, Giorgio Borin, who is passionately interested in the history of the art of cooking, discovered this recipe in a treatise by Mattia Gieger from Padua, dated 1639.

It is recommended that you choose a small duck for this recipe: The fine, tender flesh will be cooked with the fruit for a long time, thus becoming extremely succulent. Before preparing this dish you must remove the remains of the feathers on the skin, carefully passing a blowlamp or open gas flame over it. As an alternative to duck, you can use goose for this recipe. The stuffing for the bird consists of pears, halved lemons, and cherries or grapes, depending on the time of year.

Arquà Petrarca, the native village of our chef, is the home of a wonderful wine. Biancarosa Zecchin's restaurant is in the middle of the Colli Euganei vineyards, which produce an excellent, dry white wine from Cabernet grapes – perfect for quenching the braised duck, which takes two hours to cook. The fruit is pressed through a sieve to remove the pips and peel, and the resulting liquor is then added to the meat. For an even more aromatic sauce, add some of the juices that remain after braising the duck and purée with a hand-held blender. The duck is served with more fruit, sautéd in advance in butter and sugar.

Rub salt on the inside of the duck. Peel 2 pears and chop finely. Carefully peel the lemon. Wash and separate the grapes.

Stuff the duck with the pears, the quartered lemon, and the grapes. Oil a casserole dish and cook the stuffed duck for 1 hour at 465° F/240° C.

Pour the white wine over the duck. Braise in the oven for another hour.

with Fruit

As soon as the duck is cooked and golden brown, take it out of the oven and remove the fruit filling with a spoon.

Press the fruit through a sieve, reserving the sauce. Peel the remaining pear and cut into fine slices. Wash the cherries and remove the pits.

Melt the butter in a skillet and sauté the pear in it. Sauté the cherries in butter in another skillet. Sprinkle with sugar and boil to reduce. Serve the sliced duck with the fruit sauce and sautéd fruits.

Partridge

Preparation time:	*50 minutes*
Cooking time:	*40 minutes*
Difficulty:	★★

Serves 4

2	partridge or red-legged partridge
6 oz/150 g	peeled chestnuts
6 oz/150 g	small onions
	salt
	pepper
4 tbsp	vegetable oil
10	sage leaves

2 tbsp	white wine
6 oz/150 g	porcini mushrooms
1½ tbsp/20 g	butter
1 tbsp	sugar
2 tbsp	white wine vinegar
½ bunch	parsley

For the polenta:

1¼ cups/	
200 g	polenta
	coarse salt

For the garnish:

	sage leaves

In the countryside around Vicenza, where there is still a lot of hunting, there is a long tradition of cooking with wild game fowl, and you can enjoy the most wonderful dishes in the regional cuisine there, especially in winter.

Partridge or red-legged partridge, the flesh of which is reminiscent of tender chicken, is highly regarded by gourmets. Francesca de Giovannini fries the partridge first and then pours white wine over it. Depending on availability, quail, which is smaller, can be substituted for the partridge or red-legged partridge.

Francesca de Giovannini has added a personal touch to this traditional recipe by adding porcini mushrooms. These are very popular in the region and because of their strong flavor make excellent accompaniments to meat or poultry. They are frequently used in the preparation of

tasty sauces. In this recipe they combine wonderfully well with the small onions and chestnuts.

Chestnuts grow particularly well on the granite soils of southern Europe. The trees bear fruit until they are 50 years old. If you want to use fresh chestnuts, cut a cross in the shells and put them in a saucepan of boiling water with a few bay leaves; they will then be easy to peel.

In the Veneto region, serving a wild game dish without polenta would be almost unimaginable, but cornmeal is used in many other combinations as well. This is why the natives of the Veneto region and northern Italy as a whole have earned the name *polentoni*. Polenta is eaten hot, cold, boiled, or baked, and there are endless ways of preparing it. Purists still cook polenta in a copper cauldron over a wood fire.

For the polenta, heat 2 cups/500 ml water with some coarse salt in a saucepan. As soon as the water is boiling, trickle in the cornmeal. Stir with a balloon whisk and cook for about 40 minutes, stirring constantly.

Cut into the partridge along the breastbone on both sides and then divide into two pieces. Steam the chestnuts with the peeled onions for about 10 minutes.

Lay the halved partridge on a high-sided baking sheet. Season with salt and pepper. Pour over 2 tbsp vegetable oil and sprinkle over the sage leaves. Roast for 10 minutes at 400° F/200° C. Pour over the white wine and return to the oven for a further 10 minutes.

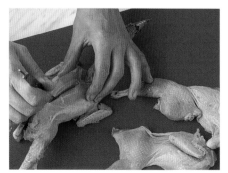

with Polenta

Heat 1 tbsp vegetable oil in a skillet and sauté the chopped porcini mushrooms for about 3 minutes.

For the sauce, heat the remaining vegetable oil in a pan with the butter and sugar, stirring with a wooden spoon.

Add the chestnuts, porcini mushrooms, and onions to the caramel sauce. Stir for 1 minute. Pour in the vinegar and continue stirring. Sprinkle with chopped parsley. Serve the partridge portions with the sauce and polenta. Garnish with sage leaves.

Braised Pigeon

Preparation time: 30 minutes
Cooking time: 50 minutes
Difficulty: ★★

Serves 4

4	oven-ready pigeons, each 1lb/400 g
7 tbsp	extra-virgin olive oil
scant ½ cup/ 100 ml	dry Marsala
scant ½ cup/ 100 ml	*vin santo*
7 tbsp	meat stock
12 oz/300 g	spinach
2 tsp/10 g	golden raisins
1 tbsp	pine nuts
	salt
	pepper

One of the attractions on the menu at the "La Mora" restaurant in Ponte a Moriano is the pigeon cooked in meat stock and sweet wine inspired by a traditional recipe. Sauro Brunicardi and his colleague Paolo Indragoli serve it with spinach, pine nuts, and raisins.

Since pigeon are rather difficult to bone, ask your butcher to do this for you. Although Sauro Brunicardi has a definite preference for pigeon, you can also use quail or partridge for this recipe.

The pigeons are quenched with Marsala and *vin santo*, which make an excellent sauce. *Vin santo* is straw-colored, very sweet, and has a smell slightly reminiscent of apples. There is a range of accredited quality *vin santo* products, all made in Tuscany: Our chef recommends *vin santo* from Montecarlo. *Vin santo* is made from dried grapes and takes up to seven years to mature, during which time it

acquires an amber color and a taste reminiscent of candied fruit.

Marsala comes from the Trapani region in northwestern Sicily. Until the late 18th century, this heavy, dark red wine was unknown beyond the island. In 1770, however, an Englishman called John Woodhouse was shipwrecked off the Sicilian coast; after he was rescued he discovered Marsala, and began producing and selling this delicious wine on a large scale himself. The best Marsala wines are matured for more than ten years in the barrel before they are sold.

The accompaniments to this dish consist essentially of crunchy green spinach leaves. It is possible to substitute Swiss chard leaves for the spinach. Our chef adds golden raisins and pine nuts, giving the dish a touch of sweetness.

Cut the pigeons in half along the breast. Remove the bones and hammer vigorously to flatten.

Heat 5 tbsp olive oil in a large pan and add the pigeon halves, browning them for about 20 minutes and turning once.

Pour in the Marsala and vin santo. Reduce over high heat for 5 minutes.

"Brunicardi"

Pour in the meat stock and reduce for a further 10–15 minutes.

Blanch the spinach leaves for a few minutes in boiling salted water. Drain.

Heat the remaining olive oil in a pan and add the spinach, golden raisins, and pine nuts. Cook for 5 minutes, then season with salt and pepper. Serve the pigeons on plates with the spinach arranged around them and some of the sauce poured on top.

Chicken

Preparation time: 1 hour
Cooking time: 1 hour 20 minutes
Difficulty: ★★

Serves 4

7 tbsp	extra-virgin olive oil
3¼ lb/1.5 kg	oven-ready chicken
	salt
	pepper
1 cup/250 ml	red wine
scant ¾ stick/80 g	butter

For the sauce:
2 cups/500 ml   red wine

scant ½ stick/50 g	butter

For the salad:

2	carrots
8 oz/200 g	cauliflower
1	red bell pepper
1 stick	celery
	vinegar
⅓ cup/50 g	black and green olives
4	anchovy fillets
	salt
	extra-virgin olive oil

For the garnish:

4	anchovy fillets, rolled

On the menu at Alfonso Caputo's restaurant on the Sorrento peninsula is an amazing chicken dish created by the chef, which is called "Limoneto Massese". With the chicken, which is braised in a sauce made from wine and butter, he serves vegetables cooked separately in order to conserve their color, flavor, and crunchy texture. This recipe successfully unites land and sea with the inclusion by Alfonso Caputo of a marine ingredient in the form of anchovy fillets.

For this recipe, our chef chooses a chicken of outstanding quality from a small producer in nearby Limoneto Massese. Before you prepare the chicken, make sure that it has been cleanly plucked. Any residual feathers should be carefully burned off with a soldering iron or open gas flame. Once you have browned the chicken, add wine and butter to the saucepan and braise for at least 40 minutes. As regards the wine, Alfonso Caputo recommends a Piedirosso from southern Italy; although its tannin content is fairly high, when reduced this wine yields quite a syrupy sauce.

The tasty salad consists mainly of peppers, cauliflower, carrots, and celery. Each of these vegetables is cooked individually for five minutes in the same water. As soon as one vegetable is cooked, it is scooped out with a slotted spoon before the next is added to the saucepan. A little wine vinegar is added to the water to stop the vegetables from losing their color during cooking; this is especially important for cauliflower, which otherwise turns a grayish color.

It is quite easy to serve this dish like a professional chef. Use a small, circular mold to arrange the salad on the plate, then decorate with a rolled anchovy fillet. The jointed chicken is garnished on the plate with the dark-colored sauce, to pleasing effect.

Heat the olive oil in a large pan (preferably copper) and place the chicken in the hot oil. Season with salt and pepper and fry on all sides for 10 minutes.

Add the red wine and butter. Cover and simmer for 40 minutes.

Peel and finely chop the carrots. Cut the cauliflower florets into quarters. Halve the bell pepper, remove the seeds and ribs, and chop finely. Cut the celery into small pieces. Blanch each vegetable for 5 minutes. Then plunge them into ice water.

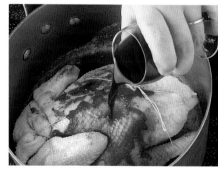

"Limoneto Massese"

Drain the vegetables and transfer to a dish with the olives and anchovies. Season with salt and drizzle a little olive oil on top.

For the sauce, reduce the wine by two-thirds in a small long-handled pan over high heat. Add the butter. Cook for another 5 minutes, stirring constantly.

Lay the cooked chicken on its back and separate the legs and wings. Remove the skin and bones. Cut the meat into even-sized pieces. Arrange the vegetables on plates and garnish with anchovy rolls. Add the chicken portions and serve with the wine sauce.

Pigeon Supreme

Preparation time: 50 minutes
Cooking time: 50 minutes
Difficulty: ★★

Serves 4

2	oven-ready pigeons, each 1¼ lb/500 g
8 oz/200 g	potatoes
	salt
	pepper
5 tbsp	olive oil
2 oz/50 g	black truffles
⅞ stick/ 100 g	butter

For the game stock:

	remains of the pigeon
1 tbsp	flour (optional)
1 tbsp	olive oil
3	shallots
1	carrot
1 sprig	rosemary
3 cloves	garlic
⅔ cup/ 150 ml	white wine

For the garnish (optional):

pomegranate seeds

In the Marche region, pigeon stuffed with potatoes was once a classic dish for serving at big family gatherings. Liver, pork, chicken, and truffles were served as an accompaniment to pigeon, which was flavored with cinnamon.

Alberto Melagrana has drawn inspiration from this traditional dish. His delicious pigeon supreme is a dish that emphasizes the refinement of Italian cuisine.

Connoisseurs love the fine, delicate flesh of wild pigeon, which is made into very sophisticated dishes. Wild pigeon is available in markets in Italy from spring to late summer; at other times of the year you will need to substitute commercially reared pigeon.

"Supreme" designates the breast of a bird, with the skin removed, together with the wing bone. If you find it difficult to joint the pigeons into supremes, ask your butcher to

do this for you. Save the remains of the birds for the stock. If you think they look too fatty, add a little flour.

In Italy, and in the Marche region in particular, truffles are regarded as the "diamonds" of gastronomy. There are many different kinds of truffle, but for the sauce in this recipe our chef recommends that you choose the black variety. Brush them carefully to remove any particles of earth and then soak for a few minutes in lukewarm water. They should be cooked in extra-virgin olive oil over low heat to retain their incomparable flavor.

To garnish this luxurious dish, Alberto Melagrana has chosen the fruit that bears his name: the pomegranate or, in Italian, *melagrana*!

Remove the legs and tips of the wings from the pigeons. Joint the birds into supremes by cutting along the breastbone on both sides. Reserve the rest of the pigeons.

For the stock, sauté the remaining meat from the pigeon with a little flour in 1 tbsp olive oil. Add the shallots, carrot, rosemary, and garlic. Pour in half the white wine. When this has reduced, add the remaining wine, top up with water, and simmer for 40 minutes.

Peel the potatoes and cut into thin slices. Cook in boiling water for 15–20 minutes. Mash with a fork. Add 2 tbsp strained stock and season with salt and pepper.

"Melagrana"

Heat 2 tbsp olive oil in a skillet. Add the mashed potatoes and fry gently.

Heat the remaining olive oil in a saucepan and brown the pigeon supremes, then transfer them to the oven and bake for 3 minutes at 340° F/170° C. Cut into slices.

Heat the strained game stock in a saucepan with the finely sliced truffles. Season with salt and pepper. Remove from the heat, add the butter, and beat with a balloon whisk. Arrange the supremes on plates with the potatoes and sauce and garnish with the pomegranate seeds.

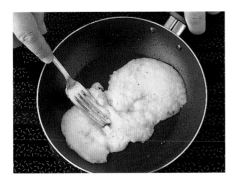

Stuffed

Preparation time: 40 minutes
Cooking time: 1 hour 5 minutes
Difficulty: ★★

Serves 4

4	oven-ready pigeons
8 slices	pancetta (or other slab bacon)
2–3	carrots
1	onion
1 stick	celery
2 cloves	garlic
1 sprig	rosemary
1	clove
2	bay leaves

	salt
	pepper

3 tbsp	olive oil
1 scant cup/ 200 ml	white wine

For the stuffing:

6 oz/150 g	ground pork
½ clove	garlic
2 sprigs	parsley
1	egg
1 tbsp	grated parmesan

For the garnish (optional):

	golden raisins
	almonds
	rosemary sprigs

In the Middle Ages, the nobility in the region around Padua used to keep pigeons in the towers of their castles. These provided an excellent reserve of food to fall back on in the event of a siege. The pigeons, which flew over the enemy in their search for food and even carried messages, always returned home.

This stuffed pigeon dish is a delicious specialty devised by Biancarosa Zecchin, who lives near Padua. The tasty stuffing consists of pork flavored with garlic, parsley, and parmesan. The pigeons are wrapped in slices of bacon and braised with vegetables. If you can, buy young pigeons with tender flesh, which do not require so much cooking.

The parmesan and egg serve to bind together the pork stuffing. Most parmesan is made in Emilia-Romagna and its production is subject to very strict controls. The city of

Parma has been famous for its cheese since medieval times. The cheeses take 18–36 months to mature.

Each stuffed pigeon is wrapped in two slices of pancetta. During cooking, the pigeon absorbs some of the flavor of the bacon, but above all it absorbs the fat, which prevents it drying out. Pancetta is available in different forms in Italy – flat or rolled, salted, dried, or smoked.

As an accompaniment to the pigeon, our chef suggests serving slices of polenta. Cook the cornmeal, stirring constantly, until it forms a thick oatmeal porridge consistency, then cool it in a dish. When it is firm, you can easily turn it out and cut it up. Garnish the pigeon with golden raisins, almonds, or fresh rosemary.

For the stuffing, place the ground meat, sliced garlic, chopped parsley, egg, and grated parmesan in a dish. Knead the mixture until it is smooth.

Stuff each pigeon with a quarter of the stuffing mixture.

Wrap each pigeon in 2 slices of pancetta and secure with kitchen string.

Pigeon

Place the sliced carrots, quartered onion, chopped celery, garlic, stuffed pigeon, rosemary, clove, bay leaves, salt, pepper, olive oil, and white wine in an ovenproof dish. Cook in a slow oven for 1 hour.

Remove the pigeons from the oven and untie the kitchen string. Remove the pancetta slices and chop finely.

Pass the sauce and vegetables through a sieve over a saucepan. Add the chopped pancetta to the pan, season to taste, and simmer for 5 minutes. Serve the pigeon on a bed of sauce with slices of polenta.

Desserts & Pastries

Bavarois

Preparation time: 20 minutes
Cooling time: 4–6 hours
Cooking time: 5 minutes
Difficulty: ✶

Serves 4

For the bavarois:

2	egg whites
6 leaves	gelatin
6 oz/150 g	acacia honey
1 cup/250 ml	light whipping cream
3½ tbsp/50 g	pine nuts

For the blueberry sauce:

8 oz/200 g	blueberries
2 tbsp/30 g	sugar

These light bavarois desserts, which were originally a northern Italian dish, taste good, even after a sumptuous main course. Sauro Brunicardi, who has a restaurant in Tuscany, combines two products from the mountains of Garfagnana in this recipe, namely honey and blueberries. For a long time now this fresh, fruity dessert has appeared on the menu at his restaurant all year round, to the delight of his guests.

Our chef varies the classic bavarois recipe by adding acacia honey, which is golden yellow, very runny, and gives the bavarois a subtle, mild flavor. Sauro Brunicardi is opposed to substituting any other kind of honey, such as chestnut honey, whose flavor would be too dominant.

The honey is heated slowly in a bain-marie or double boiler, with the gelatin then being dissolved in it. Gelatin must always be dissolved in lukewarm liquid before use.

The honey and gelatin mixture is then folded into the frothy egg whites and stirred gently to produce a smooth, firm meringue mixture. For the sauce, Sauro Brunicardi recommends puréeing the blueberries and sugar in a blender and then pressing them through a funnel-shaped sieve to obtain a smooth sauce without any skin and seeds. Instead of the blueberries you can use mildly acidic fruits such as raspberries or sour cherries, which provide a delicious contrast with the sweet bavarois.

Leave the dessert in the refrigerator to set before serving. Pour a little blueberry sauce onto the plates, remove the bavarois from the molds, and place in the center of the sauce. Pour a little honey over the top and garnish each portion with whole blueberries and a few mint leaves. Roasted pine nuts also go well with this dish.

For the bavarois, beat the egg whites until stiff. Soften the gelatin in lukewarm water.

Heat the honey in a double boiler. Add the softened gelatin leaves to the honey and stir with a spoon to dissolve them.

Remove the honey and gelatin from the double boiler and gradually fold into the beaten egg whites. Stir until the mixture has cooled.

with Honey

Whip the cream until stiff and fold gently into the meringue with 2 tbsp/30 g pine nuts. Divide between 4 molds and chill in the refrigerator for 4–6 hours.

For the blueberry sauce, purée the washed blueberries with the sugar in a blender, reserving a few for the garnish.

Pass the blueberry purée through a sieve into a small bowl. Pour the sauce onto the plates, turn the bavarois out of the molds, and place in the center. Garnish with a little honey, whole blueberries, and roasted pine nuts.

Cantucci

Preparation time:	30 minutes
Cooking time:	40 minutes
Difficulty:	☆

Serves 4–6

⅞ stick/100 g	butter
1¾ cups/	
200 g	confectioner's sugar
1 cup/200 g	sugar
1 tbsp	grated lemon peel
3	eggs

7 tbsp	blossom honey
3 cups/500 g	strong bread flour
1½ cups/	
200 g	almonds
½ tbsp/8 g	yeast
	salt

These *cantucci* are typical of the town of Prato, not far from Florence. The Italians love eating them as the perfect ending to a meal – especially if they are served with a glass of *vin santo*.

Every baker in Tuscany sells *cantucci*, which are also known as *biscotti di Prato*. Nowadays, however, they are also available throughout Italy, and even abroad. Some people like eating *cantucci* at breakfast, while others prefer them in the afternoon with a cup of hot chocolate.

The basic dough for the *cantucci* is rolled out into small baguettes, baked, and then cut into slices diagonally. These are then dried again in the oven, hence the name *biscotti*, which means "cooked twice." Since they are dried so thoroughly in the oven, they keep for a long time; earlier, when methods of preserving food were still very limited, this was especially important.

Although *cantucci* have a long tradition, they have not changed fundamentally in terms of their shape or ingredients. The almonds can be blanched and roasted or just chopped. Many fans of *cantucci* also like a subtle flavor of aniseed. Paolo Luni recommends making the dough using half ordinary sugar and half confectioner's sugar, to make the *cantucci* really crunchy.

Honey is also added to the dough as an extra refinement. In Italy, about 85,000 beekeepers offer many different kinds of honey – choose between acacia, citrus, chestnut, heather, eucalyptus, thyme, lime, and many others.

Using a balloon whisk, beat the butter in a bowl until it is light and foamy. Then add the sugar mixed with the grated lemon peel.

Break the eggs and add to the butter mixture. Mix thoroughly.

Add the honey, the flour, almonds and yeast, and a pinch of salt.

Mix thoroughly until all the flour has been incorporated and you have made a smooth dough.

Form the dough into several long, thin rolls. Place on a baking sheet and bake for 10 minutes at 430° F/220° C.

Lay the baked rolls on a chopping board. Using a knife, cut diagonally into slices about ½ in/1 cm thick. Return to the oven and dry for about 30 minutes at 265° F/130° C.

Almond

Preparation time:	20 minutes
Cooking time:	15 minutes
Difficulty:	★★

Serves 4

1 tbsp	olive oil
3½ cups/	
500 g	blanched almonds
1 cup/220 g	sugar
1	lemon

For the garnish:
bay leaves

Bridal couples in Abruzzi were traditionally served almond cracknel in the shape of a house – symbolizing the future home of the newlyweds – as the sweetmeat was supposed to bring them good luck. With the passage of time, the almond confection became known all over the Italian peninsula. In the south it is prepared mostly on Christmas Eve, but it is found at funfairs everywhere: For children, a ride on a roundabout is incomplete without it.

Back in ancient times, the Romans used to produce sweetmeats by coating almonds in honey. The oval nuts, which came from Asia, were called "Greek nuts." Many Eastern sweetmeats are made with almonds.

For this recipe you should remove the brown skin from the almonds, by blanching them for a minute in boiling water. Once they have cooled, it is easy to remove the skins by pressing between the thumb and forefinger.

To make cracknel successfully, it is essential to stir the almond and sugar mixture vigorously all the time it is on the stove, preferably with a wooden spatula. It is also advisable to cut the cracknel on a marble slab, or at least on a very smooth surface that will not be damaged by the knife. Both the work surface and the blade of the knife should be oiled to make it easier to cut the cracknel. The lemon is responsible for the lovely caramel color.

In Abruzzi, almond cracknel is always garnished with bay leaves. Natives of Abruzzi, who are great lovers of tradition, revere the bay tree: As an ancient symbol of imperial power, it is supposed to bring wealth to the household.

Using a cloth, wipe a little olive oil over the work surface and the blade of a large sharp knife.

Halve the blanched almonds and place in a pan with the sugar.

Heat the pan, stirring the contents vigorously with a wooden spatula so that the almonds and sugar bind together well. When the almonds are browned, remove the pan from the heat.

Cracknel

Carefully transfer the almond mixture to the oiled work surface.

Squeeze the lemon over the top. Using the oiled blade of the knife, form the mixture into a rectangular shape.

Cut the cracknel into even-sized pieces. Arrange on a plate and garnish with the bay leaves.

Fregolata

Preparation time:	20 minutes
Cooking time:	20 minutes
Difficulty:	★

Serves 6

1¼ cups/	
200 g	strong wheat flour
3½ tbsp/50 g	yellow cornmeal
	salt
1⅓ cups/	
150 g	confectioner's sugar
1 small	
packet	yeast

1⅓ cups/	
150 g	blanched ground
	almonds
¼	unwaxed lemon
1	vanilla pod
1¼ sticks/	
150 g	butter
2	egg yolks
	oil for the baking pan

For the garnish:

	almonds

Fregolata was originally enjoyed by sweet-toothed inhabitants of Mantua in Lombardy before it became known all over northern Italy. At the end of a meal, or at convivial gatherings, each person breaks off a piece of this hard, crumbly cake and dips it in a glass of Tuscan *vin santo*. In Italy, it is also commonly eaten in small wine bars, which are called *enoteca* in Italian.

According to Paolo Luni, the word *fregolata* is derived from the dialect word *friabile*, meaning "fragile." Although easy to prepare yourself, it is available in patisseries all year round. If you have not had time to buy any, the necessary ingredients are always to hand in your store cupboard. Another advantage is that *fregolata* keeps for about two months.

The basic ingredients of *fregolata* are wheat flour and yellow cornmeal, which is also used for making polenta. Since cornmeal has a low gluten content, the resulting dough has a slightly crumbly consistency. For this reason wheat flour has to be used as well, otherwise the *fregolata* will not be successful.

After all the ingredients have been thoroughly combined, the dough must be rubbed between the fingers until a crumbly mixture is formed. The dough is then pressed into a baking pan and baked until golden yellow.

Spoon the flour into a heap on the work surface. Make a hollow in the middle for the cornmeal, a pinch of salt, the confectioner's sugar, and the yeast.

Add the almonds, grated lemon peel, inside of the vanilla pod, softened butter, and egg yolks.

Mix the ingredients well with the hands. Then rub the mixture between your fingers until a crumbly mixture is formed.

Lightly oil a round, flat baking pan and dust with flour. Spread the dough evenly in the pan using a dough scraper or with your hands.

Firm the dough in the pan by pressing with your fingertips.

Arrange a few almonds in a circle in the middle. Bake in the oven for 20 minutes at 350° F/180° C until golden yellow. Leave to cool before serving.

Venetian

Preparation time:	20 minutes
Soaking time:	1 hour
Cooking time:	10 minutes
Difficulty:	★

Serves 4

⅓ cup/50 g	golden raisins
4 tbsp	grappa
1¼ cups/ 300 ml	milk
½ stick/60 g	butter
1 pinch	salt

1½ cups/ 240 g	strong bread flour
½	unwaxed lemon
3	eggs
2	egg whites
4 tsp/20 g	pine nuts
	vegetable oil for deep frying
1 scant cup/ 100 g	confectioner's sugar

The Venetians have always had a reputation for being particularly fond of celebrations and the sweetmeats served on such occasions. Carnival time in Venice used to last several months and was always the excuse for feasts. Men and women wearing the *bauta*, a folk costume consisting of a three-cornered hat, black veil, and white face mask, bought a wide variety of sweetmeats, for example fritters made from choux pastry, called *fritelle* or *fritole*, or other fried tidbits. Now these delicacies are available all year round.

In the 18th century, fritter sellers were an integral part of the landscape of the city of Venice. In his play *Il Campiello*, the Venetian playwright Carlo Goldoni, who reformed the Italian theater, actually gave the main role to a woman selling fritters.

A classic choux pastry, enhanced with raisins and pine kernels and fried in olive oil, forms the basis for this recipe.

It does not contain any sugar, since this could caramelize and the fritters would then be too dark in color. As soon as the butter, flour, and milk mixture comes away from the bottom of the saucepan, remove the pan from the heat. Transfer the dough to a work surface and leave it to cool. The eggs must not be beaten into the mixture while it is hot, because they would curdle and ruin the dough. As an added refinement, pour in a little grappa or aniseed liqueur.

In order to determine whether the oil has reached the right temperature, sprinkle in a little flour or a few drops of water. If bubbles rise to the surface, the temperature is perfect. Use your finger to push the dough off the spoon into the oil. It will soon be transformed into small, golden-yellow balls. Drain them on paper towels, coat in sugar, and eat cold.

Immerse the raisins in the grappa. Mix the milk and butter with a pinch of salt in a saucepan. Bring to the boil.

As soon as the milk boils, add the flour and the grated lemon peel. Stir until the dough comes away from the bottom of the saucepan. Place the dough on a heatproof work surface and leave to cool.

Transfer the dough to a bowl. Add the 3 eggs and the egg whites. Stir vigorously to bind the eggs fully into the dough.

Fritters

Add the soaked raisins and the pine nuts. Give the mixture a final stir.

Heat the oil in a skillet. Using a soup spoon, place small portions of dough in the oil. As soon as the fritters begin to rise, turn them so they become golden yellow all over.

Drain the fritters on paper towels. Dust with confectioner's sugar and serve cold.

Little Chocolate Cakes

Preparation time:	30 minutes
Freezing time:	12 hours
Cooking time:	15 minutes
Difficulty:	★

Serves 4

2¼ sticks/	
255 g	butter
10 oz/250 g	semisweet chocolate
¾ cup/160 g	sugar
6	eggs
1¼ cups/	
145 g	flour
1 tbsp/16 g	dried yeast

1 packet	vanilla sugar
4	unwaxed oranges

For the syrup:
3½ tbsp/50 g   sugar

For the garnish (optional):
mint leaves

These sophisticated little chocolate cakes, originally a specialty from Milan, have since become famous far beyond the borders of Lombardy. Alberto Melagrana, a great chocolate aficionado, has refined this recipe with the addition of oranges and has thus created a culinary delight.

You need patience to melt chocolate in a bain-marie or double boiler; it only works if you stir constantly, otherwise lumps form. Cocoa spread rapidly all over Europe after the conquistadors brought it back with them from the New World, and cafés in Florence and Venice were offering their customers chocolate as early as the 17th century. The special interest that is taken by the natives of Turin and Piedmont in this exotic delicacy also dates back to those times.

Cocoa is obtained from the fruit of the cocoa tree, which can grow to a height of over 25 feet/8 meters. The cocoa beans are first fermented, then roasted and ground to create the dark, powdery chocolate mass from which chocolate is then made.

Our chef serves orange sauce with these little chocolate cakes. Oranges are cultivated mainly in Calabria and Sicily, and in this recipe they complement beautifully the flavor of the chocolate. Alberto Melagrana recommends that you use top-quality navel oranges, which are harvested between November and February. They have practically no pips and are recognizable by their thick, coarse peel, which is easily removed. Their juicy flesh is ideal for making sauces. When buying, choose shiny fruit that feel heavy. As they are not particularly delicate, they can be kept for several days at room temperature.

Melt all but a small knob of butter in a double boiler, stirring with a balloon whisk. Add the chocolate, broken into pieces, and stir to combine.

Remove the butter and chocolate from the double boiler and stir the sugar into the chocolate mixture. Add the eggs, stirring constantly. Gradually stir in all but 1 tsp/5 g of the sieved flour, the yeast, and the vanilla sugar.

Grease 4 small baking pans with the remaining butter, dust with the remaining flour, and fill with the chocolate mixture. Cover with plastic wrap and place in the freezer for 12 hours.

with Orange Sauce

Wash the oranges thoroughly and peel thinly with a knife. Squeeze the fruit and reserve the juice.

Cut the orange peel into thin strips. To prepare the syrup, add the sugar to 1¼ cups/300 ml water and bring to the boil.

Add the orange peel to the liquid and simmer for 10 minutes. Bake the chocolate cakes for 10 minutes at 340° F/170° C, then remove from the pans. Pour some of the orange syrup and juice onto each plate, then place a chocolate cake in the middle. Garnish with mint leaves.

Mirabelle

Preparation time: 40 minutes
Cooking time: 30 minutes
Difficulty: ★★

Serves 4

1½ lb/600 g   potatoes
10 oz/250 g   flour
1   egg
               salt
1¾ sticks/
200 g   butter

2 cups/
100 g   fresh breadcrumbs
2 pinches   ground cinnamon
3 tbsp   confectioner's sugar
10   red mirabelle plums
               salt

The popularity of mirabelle *gnocchi* as a dessert extends from Trentino to Friuli, and even to Slovenia. All these regions have belonged at some time in their history to the Austro-Hungarian Empire, and Bohemian chefs often cooked for the nobility when they were staying in their castles in Trieste. These chefs brought with them their own culinary specialties, which as a result became well known in Italy too.

Gnocchi normally consist of potatoes and wheat flour or maize flour, or a mixture of flour and ricotta cheese. Floury varieties of potato, such as bintje, are particularly suitable for making *gnocchi*, which are now famous far beyond Italy's borders. They are usually cooked briefly in salted water and then served with butter, cheese, or a tomato sauce. A fruit filling is therefore rather exotic.

Excellent mirabelles grow in the countryside around Trieste, and are eaten raw or made into schnapps. The variety called *Violine* is very popular for cooking, while the yellow and orange-colored fruit are eaten raw. The *gnocchi* will keep their shape better if you use fresh fruit, as frozen fruit produces too much juice. Damsons, dried apricots, or cherries can be used instead of mirabelles in this recipe.

The hot *gnocchi* are sprinkled with sugar and cinnamon and a sauce, made from breadcrumbs and melted butter, is then poured over them. The hot butter melts the sugar, so that the *gnocchi* look as though they have been caramelized. In Friuli, hot mirabelle *gnocchi* are often served with a goulash, but are also eaten as a dessert.

Boil the unpeeled potatoes for 20 minutes. Leave to cool and remove the skins. Cut into large cubes and press firmly through a sieve to form a purée.

Spoon a third of the flour onto a work surface. Transfer the potato purée onto the floured surface and make a hollow in the middle. Break an egg into the hollow and sprinkle a little salt on top. Knead with the hands, gradually working in the flour until you have a smooth dough.

Melt ⅞ stick/100 g butter in a pan, sprinkle in 1½ cups/80 g breadcrumbs, and mix with a wooden spatula. Stir in a pinch of cinnamon and 2 tsp confectioner's sugar.

Gnocchi

Cut open the mirabelles and remove the pits. Using a spoon, fill the fruit with the breadcrumb mixture and squeeze the plums so they close.

Divide the dough into portions the size of an egg and form into circles with your hands. Place a mirabelle in the middle of each circle and enclose it in the dough. Roll the dough into a ball.

Cook the gnocchi for 5 minutes in boiling water, then remove with a slotted spoon. Brown the remaining breadcrumbs in ⅞ stick/100 g butter in a skillet. Arrange the gnocchi on plates, dust with confectioner's sugar and cinnamon, and top with the hot breadcrumbs.

Gubana

Preparation time: 1 hour
Soaking the raisins: 1 hour
Resting time (dough): 3 hours
Cooking time: 50 minutes
Difficulty: ★★★

Serves 4–6

For the dough, first stage:
¾ stick/90 g   butter
2 tbsp/30 g   fresh yeast
⅜ cup/90 g   sugar
10   eggs
6 cups/700 g   flour

For the dough, second stage:
8 cups/900 g   flour
¾ cup/180 g   sugar

1⅝ sticks/180 g butter
3½ tbsp/50 g   honey
1   unwaxed lemon
1   unwaxed orange
10   eggs

1   vanilla pod
scant ½ cup/
100 ml   Marsala
1 tbsp/15 g   salt

For the filling:
⅔ cup/100 g   roasted almonds
½ cup/50 g   walnuts
⅔ cup/150 g   crushed amaretti cookies
2 tbsp/50 g   each pine nuts,
                   chocolate strands,
                   sugar, cocoa powder
1½ cups/250 g   raisins soaked in scant
                   ½ cup/100 ml grappa
6½ tbsp/100 g   apricot jam

1   egg white
                 sugar

Gubana originated in Friuli and Venezia Giulia, in the province of Gorizia. This golden yellow brioche has a sumptuous filling of dried fruit, crushed amaretti cookies, chocolate, and jam, and is made in the shape of a snail. It is served as a dessert, usually with plum liqueur.

The preparation of the dough, which takes place in two stages, seems rather complicated at first glance, but the interval of one hour between the two stages gives you time for a rest. To raise the dough more quickly, you can put it in a bowl, cover it with a cloth, and put it in a pre-warmed oven, leaving the door open. If it is too stiff to knead, just add a dash of water or white wine. Although the dough has hardly any regional variations, the filling is quite a different matter, with everyone having their own personal preferences. As a general rule, however, the raisins are soaked in grappa, or alternatively schnapps made from

damson plums. Paolo Luni advises against substituting dried plums or apricots for the raisins.

The amaretti cookies, which are produced mainly in Lombardy and Liguria, give the filling a crunchy texture and a highly characteristic flavor. These small, round macaroons consist of chopped almonds, sugar, egg white, and a liqueur made from bitter almonds. In Italy, amaretti are often served with a cup of coffee, but they are also used for sweet dishes.

In this recipe, the filling is rolled in the dough and the roll is then wound into the shape of a snail. *Gubana* tastes especially good for breakfast, preferably dipped in hot chocolate. If it is wrapped carefully, it will keep for four or five days.

For the first stage of preparing the dough, knead the butter with the hands to soften. Place the dissolved yeast, sugar, 7 egg yolks, 3 whole eggs, the flour, and the soft butter in a bowl. Knead with the hands, form the dough into a ball, and leave to rise for an hour.

For the second stage, spoon the flour onto a work surface and make a hollow in the middle. Add the sugar, butter, honey, grated lemon and orange peels, 7 egg yolks, 3 whole eggs, the inside of the vanilla pod, the Marsala, and the salt.

Place the risen dough on top of these ingredients and gradually incorporate the flour and the other ingredients, working from the inside outwards. Knead everything thoroughly, form into a ball and leave the dough to rise for 1 hour.

For the filling, mix the roasted almonds with the other nuts. Mix together in a bowl the crushed amaretti cookies, nuts, pine nuts, chocolate strands, sugar, cocoa, drained raisins, and apricot jam.

Roll out the dough on a floured work surface to form a large rectangle. Spread the filling out along the center and roll the dough up lengthways.

Wind the roll into the shape of a snail's shell. Cover and leave to rise for another hour, then transfer to an oiled baking sheet. Brush with egg white and sprinkle with sugar. Bake for 50 minutes in a preheated oven at 330° F/165° C.

Tiramisù

Preparation time:	*45 minutes*
Difficulty:	✷✷

Serves 4

2	eggs
	salt
8 tsp/40 g	sugar
½ tsp	vanilla essence
10 oz/250 g	mascarpone

2 shots	double espresso
2 tbsp	brandy
4	ladyfingers
2 tsp/10 g	cocoa powder

For the garnish:

	bitter chocolate

Tiramisù is the best-known Italian dessert of all. A veritable cult has grown up around it on the Italian peninsula, and every region, from north to south, claims to have invented this famous dish, whose name literally means "pull me up."

For the natives of Piedmont, there is no doubt: The ladyfinger cookies, called *savoiardi*, prove that the dessert was invented in their part of the country. This is disputed in Lombardy, where the natives remind everyone that mascarpone is a specialty of their region. The Romans, meanwhile, regard the dish as typical of their city. And our chef? She proudly maintains that *tiramisù* originated in the Veneto region, in the city of Vicenza.

This nutritious classic of Italian cookery is prepared in different ways in different regions. In many families, the cream is not sprinkled with cocoa powder, but is covered with fruit: for instance, peaches, bananas, or pineapple. Other variants feature different kinds of alcohol: Although in most cases Sicilian Marsala is the preferred choice for soaking the cookies, brandy, cognac, and rum are the popular alternatives.

By contrast, *tiramisù* without mascarpone is unthinkable. This delicate cream cheese is made from the cream of cow's milk, and sometimes also from buffalo milk. The milk is heated to 75–90 degrees Fahrenheit/25–32 degrees Celsius and lemon juice or white wine vinegar is added to accelerate the coagulation process. It has a fat content of 50 percent.

The espresso gives the *tiramisù* a slightly bitter tang. Espresso has been drunk in Italy since the 16th century and is sold as *caffè* on virtually every street corner.

Put 2 egg whites in a bowl with a pinch of salt. Set the yolks aside in another bowl. Beat the egg whites until frothy with a balloon whisk.

Beat the egg yolks thoroughly with the sugar and vanilla.

Fold the mascarpone into the egg yolk mixture and combine well.

Gently fold in the beaten egg whites. Spoon some of the mascarpone cream into each of 4 glasses.

Mix the espresso and brandy together in a shallow bowl. Briefly dip the ladyfingers in the coffee and brandy, break them, and divide between the glasses.

Top up the glasses with the mascarpone cream. Sprinkle with cocoa powder and garnish with chocolate.

Ravioli

Preparation time: 1 hour
Cooking time: 15 minutes
Difficulty: ☆

Serves 4

3½ cups/
400 g | blanched chestnuts
4 oz/100 g | semisweet chocolate
⅓ cup/80 g | acacia honey
½ | unwaxed mandarin orange
2 tbsp | milk
 | flour for dusting
 | oil for deep frying

For the ravioli dough:
12 oz/300 g | flour
5 tbsp | olive oil
 | salt
2 | eggs
scant ½ cup/
100 g | sugar
½ | unwaxed mandarin orange

For the garnish:
 | mandarin zest
 | walnuts

The Fischetti sisters have inherited from their *mamma* the gift of preparing wonderful dishes. Michelina Fischetti, affectionately known as "Lina," and her sister, Maria, employ their talents for the benefit of their guests in the family restaurant. They regard themselves as custodians of culinary traditions, and on this basis devise new recipes that are heavily influenced by the characteristics of Campagna cuisine.

As is customary in the region, they love cooking pasta dishes. Michelina's dish of ravioli stuffed with chestnut cream has already acquired legendary status and is frequently served on festive occasions.

The delicate flavor of mandarin oranges, which originated in China, also contributes to the success of this dessert. The flesh of the mandarin is aromatic and less acidic than that of other citrus fruits. Mandarins are available from January to April, and are mainly cultivated in Sicily. Buy heavy specimens with glossy, unblemished peel.

For a change, the chef suggests that you substitute a filling made from ricotta, honey, chocolate, and sour cherries for the chestnut cream.

For the filling, purée the chestnuts. Melt the chocolate in a bain-marie or double boiler.

Transfer the chestnut purée to a bowl. Add half the honey, all the melted chocolate and mix everything with a fork.

Grate the peel of the whole mandarin. Add half to the chestnut purée with 2 tbsp milk, mix to a smooth cream, and set aside for later.

"Lina and Maria"

For the ravioli, place the flour, olive oil, and salt in a bowl. Add the eggs, sugar, and the rest of the grated mandarin peel. Knead into a dough.

Dust the work surface with flour and roll out the dough to a rectangle 1/10 in/2mm thick. Place small amounts of filling at regular intervals on one half of the dough and cover with the other half. Cut out the ravioli with a circular cutter.

Press around the edges of the ravioli with a fork. Fry in oil until golden yellow, then drain on paper towels and transfer to plates. Drizzle over the remaining honey and garnish with mandarin zest and chopped walnuts.

Panna

Preparation time:	20 minutes
Cooling time:	5 hours
Cooking time:	20 minutes
Difficulty:	★

Serves 4

6 leaves	gelatin
2 cups/500 ml	milk
6 oz/150 g	sugar
1 cup/250 ml	heavy cream

For the coffee sauce:

½ cup/125 g	sugar
scant ½ cup/ 100 ml	espresso
1 scant cup/ 200 ml	light cream

For the chocolate sauce:

⅜ stick/40 g	butter
10 oz/250 g	dark chocolate
1 scant cup/ 200 ml	light cream

For the garnish:

mint leaves

The world-famous dessert *panna cotta* comes from the Aosta valley and is extremely popular in the northern regions of Italy. It is easy to prepare, but its success depends heavily on the quality of the ingredients used.

It is best to use Italian cream, as this has a very high fat content and is the crucial ingredient in this dish. Until the end of the 19th century, this was prepared by cooling milk for 24 hours and then skimming off the cream. Today it is produced in dairies with the aid of milk centrifuges. If you cannot obtain Italian cream, replace the milk with cream and use an extra leaf of gelatin.

Gelatin is also important for a good *panna cotta*. This colorless, odorless substance is extracted from the bones and cartilage of animals and certain algae, and can be bought in the form of powder or transparent leaves. The leaves must first be soaked in lukewarm water and then dissolved in hot liquid.

Sergio Pais serves *panna cotta* with coffee and chocolate sauce, but you can also serve it with a sauce made from a variety of fruits.

In the Orient, coffee has been known since the Middle Ages, but it was not introduced into Italy until the 15th century. The merchants of northern Italy had huge consignments of coffee brought to Trieste. The popularity of this new drink soon escalated, to a point at which the city fathers decided to restrict the number of establishments where the beverage could be served. In Italy today practically no other drink is as ubiquitous as espresso. It has a strong, slightly bitter flavor and is always topped by a delicate, light-brown layer of foam.

Place the gelatin leaves in a small bowl with lukewarm water. Bring the milk and sugar to the boil in a saucepan.

Squeeze the gelatin leaves, stir into the milk with a balloon whisk, and cook for about 3 minutes.

Pour in the cream. Bring to the boil and cook for 1 minute, stirring constantly. Pour the mixture into 4 molds and chill for 5 hours.

Cotta

For the chocolate sauce, melt the butter and chocolate in a bain-marie or double boiler, stirring constantly. Pour in the cream. Stir and set aside.

For the coffee sauce, dissolve the sugar in the espresso in a saucepan and cook for 4 minutes.

Stir the cream into the coffee sauce. Turn the panna cotta out of the molds and place each one in the middle of a plate. Pour the chocolate sauce and coffee sauce around the panna cotta and garnish with mint leaves.

Pazientina

Preparation time: 40 minutes
Cooking time for
  the Spanish bread: 30 minutes
Cooking time for
  the Brescia dough: 30 minutes
Cooking time
  for the zabaglione: 10 minutes
Difficulty: ★★★

Serves 4–6

For the Spanish bread:

7	eggs
1 scant cup/ 210 g	sugar
1¼ cups/210 g	strong bread flour
3½ tbsp/50 g	cornstarch
4 tsp/20 ml	Grand Marnier

For the Brescia dough:

1½ cups/200 g	almonds
⅞ cup/200 g	sugar
1¾ sticks/200 g	butter
1⅛ cups/200 g	strong bread flour
1 tsp/5 g	dried yeast

For the zabaglione:

10	egg yolks
⅔ cup/150 g	sugar
¼ cup/40 g	strong bread flour
1 cup/250 ml	Marsala

For the garnish:

| | chocolate leaves (or chocolate strands) |

Pazientina is something of a mascot for Paolo Luni, having for many years been a leader in his patisserie in the city center of Padua. This master pastry chef, who uses the best recipes handed down by his father and grandfather, offers regional specialties, Italian classics, and his own creations. The *pazientina* he presents here was already famous in the 19th century: Its praises were sung by the novelist Stendhal, who tried it in the "Café Pedrocchi."

Paolo Luni believes that the name *pazientina* is derived from *pazienza*, meaning "patience"; this fabulous dessert should be savored with patience, in other words slowly, although one could easily be overcome by the urge to gulp it down. Who, after all, could resist a cake like this?

Brescia dough owes its name to the eponymous city in Lombardy. Its secret lies in the fact that it consists of equal parts of flour, sugar, and butter. The chef decides how many almonds to add. When baked, it produces a really firm biscuit, chestnut brown in color.

If you have never made *zabaglione* before, Paolo Luni suggests that you place the saucepan in a bain-marie or double boiler, so that the egg yolks combine gradually with the other ingredients without forming lumps. *Zabaglione* is traditionally made with Marsala, a famous Sicilian wine, but dry white wine can also be used.

For the garnish, Paolo Luni makes chocolate leaves from chocolate, water, and glucose, which you can pour onto a marble slab in leaf shapes, cool, and then remove from the slab; alternatively they can be made using a pasta machine.

For the Spanish bread, beat 5 whole eggs, 2 egg yolks, and the sugar together in a bowl using a balloon whisk. Stir in the flour and cornstarch. Place in a 10 in/25 cm spring-form cake pan lined with baking parchment and bake for 30 minutes at 350° F/180° C.

For the Brescia dough, mix the almonds and sugar in a food processor. Add the butter, cut into pieces, and process again. Then add the flour and yeast, and knead until a ball of dough is formed.

Roll out the dough on a floured work surface. Cut out 2 circles 10 in/25 cm in diameter. Transfer the circles to a baking sheet and cook in the oven for 30 minutes at 340° F/170° C.

For the zabaglione, place 10 egg yolks in a pan. Add the sugar and flour, beating constantly. Heat the Marsala and stir into the mixture. Continue to stir over a very low heat, or in a double boiler, until the consistency of thick cream is reached. Leave to cool.

Spread a third of the zabaglione on a circle of the Brescia dough and smooth with a palette knife. If necessary, cut a thin layer from the top of the Spanish bread to level it off.

Place the Spanish bread on top of the zabaglione and brush with Grand Marnier. Spread with another third of the zabaglione and cover with the remaining circle of Brescia dough. Spread the rest of the zabaglione over the top and sides of the cake. Cover with chocolate leaves.

Pinza

Preparation time: 45 minutes
Cooking time: 1 hour 30 minutes
Difficulty: ★★

Serves 6

1 cup/250 ml	milk
¾ cup/125 g	pre-cooked yellow cornmeal
¼ stick/25 g	butter
1½ cups/175 g	confectioner's sugar
5	apples
1	pear

⅓ cup/50 g	dried figs
1	egg
⅓ cup/50 g	golden raisins
½ cup/75 g	wheat flour
1 pack	dried yeast
1 pinch	fennel seeds
4 tbsp	cognac
	salt to taste

For the garnish (optional):

	honey
	walnuts

Biancarosa Zecchin's restaurant "La Montanella" in Arquà Petrarca, near Padua, owes its success not least to her wonderful cakes. Special mention should be given to her *pinza*, an unusual cake made from cornmeal and fruit, which is ideal for a large family. *Pinza* is easy to prepare and is known to have been baked by Italian housewives since the early 19th century, using whatever fruit was available in the garden.

For this recipe, choose very fine yellow cornmeal. Purists will assure you that only classic polenta is good enough for this recipe, but then you need the patience to stand by the stove for 45 minutes, stirring until the consistency of thick oatmeal porridge is reached. For pre-cooked polenta, 20 minutes will suffice. Cornmeal used to be one of the staple foods in the rural Veneto region, and was served with every meal.

A tip that will make it easier to produce a smooth dough is to change the order of the ingredients slightly: First add the butter, then the sugar, next the cornmeal, the yeast, and finally the salt to the milk. Mix everything thoroughly before stirring in the fruit, egg, fennel seeds, and cognac. You can substitute a liquor of your choice for the cognac. Because of its strong flavor, fennel is sometimes replaced by aniseed in this recipe.

Biancarosa Zecchin advises lining the baking pan with oiled aluminum foil before filling with the dough. This prevents the cake from sticking and makes it easy to turn out. If you can, prepare the dough in advance and let it rest for a while; this will allow the flavors to develop better and the cake will be easier to cut. *Pinza* can be kept in the refrigerator for four to five days.

Bring the milk and 1 cup/250 ml water to the boil in a saucepan. Trickle in the cornmeal, stirring constantly.

Stir vigorously on the stove for 20 minutes until you have a beautiful, pale-yellow mixture.

Transfer the mixture to a bowl and add the butter, cut into pieces, and the sugar. Stir well with a large spoon to combine.

"Biancarosa"

Peel and core the apples and pear and chop into small pieces.

Add the fruit to the polenta. Mix gently.

Stir the chopped figs with the remaining ingredients into the dough. Butter the cake pan, dust with flour, and fill with the cake mixture. Bake for 1 hour 10 minutes at 350° F/180° C until crisp and golden yellow. Garnish with honey and nuts. Leave to cool before serving.

Presnitz

Preparation time:	1 hour
Resting time (dough):	30 minutes
Cooking time:	55 minutes
Difficulty:	★★★

Serves 4

For the apple purée:

4	green apples
⅜ cup/80 g	sugar
1 scant cup/ 200 ml	white wine
½	unwaxed lemon

For the dough:

12 oz/300 g	flour
2 tsp/10 g	fresh beer yeast

½ stick/60 g	butter
1	unwaxed lemon
7 tbsp	milk

2 tbsp/30 g	confectioner's sugar
2	eggs
	salt to taste

For the filling:

1	untreated orange
4 tsp/20 g	bitter chocolate shavings
¼ cup/50 g	sugar
4 tsp/20 g	honey
½ cup/60 g	walnut kernels
½ cup/80 g	raisins soaked in 2 tbsp brandy
4 tsp/20 g	crumbled dry cookies

For the garnish:

	apple balls
	orange peel

At Christmas and Easter time, everyone in Friuli looks forward to *presnitz*, a regional specialty. It contains a delicious filling of raisins, chocolate, nuts, and orange, and resembles Viennese *Apfelstrudel*. In Friuli and Venezia Giulia, in fact, two culinary traditions come together: firstly, the culinary heritage of the Austro-Hungarian Empire, and secondly the dishes with a high fat content eaten by the mountain-dwellers. Presnitz is usually sprinkled with crushed nuts and brown sugar. Here, in Paolo Zoppolatti's own variant of the recipe (*a modo mio*, or "my style"), he suggests serving the cake in the form of medallions on a green apple purée.

Begin by preparing the apple purée, making sure that the apples, which provide a fresh, slightly acidic accompaniment to the sweet cake, do not become completely soft in the pre-made syrup.

Although the numerous ingredients are combined in a blender, the dough needs additional and thorough kneading by hand. It should then be rolled out as thinly as possible with a rolling pin.

For the filling, you should preferably choose sweet, dry cookies, for example butter cookies, which are easy to crumble, but you can also use crumbled brioche.

The cake is cooked in the manner that is customary in Trieste. After you have rolled up the filling in the dough, wrap the roll in a kitchen towel or aluminum foil and poach it in water. This keeps the cake quite pale in color. Alternatively, you can roll the dough into a snail shape, like the bakers in Udine, brush it with beaten egg white, and then bake it in the oven for 40 minutes until it is golden brown.

For the apple purée, peel, core, and chop 3 apples. Heat the sugar, white wine, and the juice and peel of half a lemon in a saucepan to make a syrup. Add the apples and cook for about 20 minutes. Then purée and set aside.

For the dough, place the flour, crumbled yeast, softened butter, grated lemon peel, milk, sugar, eggs, and salt in a blender and mix until smooth. Leave to rise for about 30 minutes.

For the filling, place the grated orange peel, chocolate shavings, sugar, honey, chopped walnuts, raisins, and crumbled cookies in a bowl and mix well.

"My Style"

Spread a dish cloth on the work surface. Place the dough on it and roll out. Spread the filling on the dough and smooth with a plastic spatula.

Roll up the dough carefully, using the dish cloth. Twist the ends of the cloth and secure with kitchen string.

Place the cake, wrapped in the cloth, in an ovenproof dish filled with boiling, salted water and poach for 30 minutes. Pour off the water and remove the cloth. Cut the cake into thin slices and serve on the apple purée. Decorate with apple balls and orange peel.

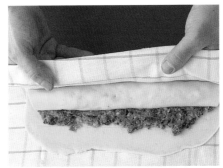

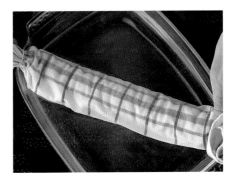

Frozen Zabaglione

Preparation time:	40 minutes
Freezing time:	12 hours
Cooking time:	1 minute
Difficulty:	★★

Serves 4

⅔ cup/150 g	sugar
6	egg yolks
3 scant cups/ 700 ml	almond milk
3¼ cups/ 800 ml	Marsala

1 cup/250 ml	cream
1 scant cup/ 100 g	crushed almonds
	knob of butter

For the garnish:

	strawberries
	chocolate curls
	almonds
	mint leaves

Frozen *zabaglione* with Marsala is a typically Italian delicacy. It is an extremely sophisticated ice cream that has become famous all over the world. People have been enjoying it since the 16th century and it used to be served to bridal couples for breakfast after their wedding night, in order to revive them!

Zabaglione is highly nutritious and is normally eaten lukewarm. The natives of Turin claim to have invented this foaming dish; in any event, they are certainly responsible for the addition of Marsala. In Piedmont, the origins of *zabaglione* are disputed. Many people maintain it was invented by the Renaissance chef Bartolomeo Scappi, while others claim it was actually the brainchild of St. Pasquale Bayon, who was chosen by the inhabitants of Turin in 1722 as the patron saint of chefs. Supporters of this theory argue that his name in the Piedmont dialect, pronounced "sanbajun," then became *zabagliun*.

Zabaglione is easy to prepare, but true success depends on the Marsala. This Sicilian wine became widespread thanks to the Englishman John Woodhouse, who was shipwrecked off Marsala on the Sicilian coast in 1770. When he tasted the local wine after his rescue, he decided to start making it to compete with Spanish sherry and Madeira. Each year, Admiral Nelson ordered 500 barrels for the English fleet in the Mediterranean and, with their victory over the French and Spanish at Trafalgar, Woodhouse rebranded the wine as "Marsala Victory Wine" – thus significantly contributing to its success.

You can garnish the frozen *zabaglione* with almonds or hazelnuts. The strawberries can be substituted with other fruit, according to the season.

Put the sugar and egg yolks in a dish suitable for a bain-marie or double boiler and heat a saucepan of water.

Stir the egg yolks and sugar with a wooden spatula until foaming.

Add the almond milk, stirring constantly.

with Marsala

Place the bowl containing the egg mixture over the saucepan of boiling water. Stir in the Marsala. Leave for 1 minute and continue stirring gently, then remove from the saucepan.

Pour the cream into a bowl and beat vigorously with a balloon whisk.

Add the cream to the egg mixture. Gradually add the crushed almonds. Pour the mixture into a buttered mold and place in the freezer for 12 hours. Slice the zabaglione and decorate with the strawberries, chocolate curls, almonds, and mint leaves.

Carrot

Preparation time: 25 minutes
Cooking time: 30 minutes
Difficulty: ☆

Serves 4–6

8 oz/200 g	carrots
2¼ sticks/270 g	butter
1⅛ cup/250 g	sugar
3	eggs
2 tsp/10 g	dried yeast
1¾ cups/300 g	strong bread flour
2 tbsp	Strega (or another herb liqueur)
1¾ cups/200 g	ground almonds
½	unwaxed lemon
1 tsp/5 g	salt
1¾ cup/250 g	whole, blanched almonds

This carrot cake is typical of South Tyrol. In the mountainous region near the Austrian border, which during the course of history has changed ownership with successive invasions and has belonged first to one country, then another, eating habits have remained staunchly resistant to change. Skiers relaxing on the slopes of the Dolomites love to restore their energy with these rich cakes and pastries, which are full of butter and almonds.

It may seem unusual to bake a cake using carrot, but its flavor is not dominant, it simply adds decorative touches of orange to the mixture. You can either grate the carrot by hand or shred it coarsely in a blender.

The almonds make the cake soft and moist. Paolo Luni claims that Apulia produces the best almonds in Italy. His personal preference is for Bari almonds, because of their mild taste.

Strega liqueur enhances the flavor of the cake and has been a popular drink in Italy for 150 years. It is dark yellow in color and is now made by only one company, based in the province of Benevent. The recipe for this exclusive drink, the manufacture of which involves various wild herbs, is kept a strict secret. Strega is drunk as bitters or is used to enhance desserts.

Decorate the cake while it is in the pan, arranging a circle of blanched almonds around the edge. Using your finger, draw a spiral in the cake mixture and arrange more almonds along the line. You can then serve the cake with cream for afternoon tea or coffee.

Cut off the ends of the carrots, peel them, then grate coarsely.

Beat together 2⅛ sticks/250 g soft butter and the sugar in a bowl, using a balloon whisk. Add the eggs.

Mix the yeast with the flour and stir into the butter and sugar mixture.

Cake

Mix in the carrot thoroughly.

Stir in the Strega liqueur, ground almonds, the grated lemon peel, and a pinch of salt.

Butter the baking pan and dust with flour. Scrape the cake mixture out of the bowl into the pan and spread evenly over the base. Decorate with blanched almonds. Bake for 30 minutes at 375° F/190° C.

Ricotta

Preparation time: 45 minutes
Cooling time: 1 hour
Cooking time: 50 minutes
Difficulty: ★★

Serves 4–6

For the dough:

⅞ cup/200 g	sugar
1¾ sticks/200 g	butter
4	eggs
½	unwaxed lemon
1	vanilla pod
2½ cups/400 g	strong bread flour

1 tsp/5 g   baking powder

For the cream:

1 scant cup/200 ml	milk
½	unwaxed lemon
¼ cup/50 g	sugar
2	egg yolks
2 tbsp/30 g	strong bread flour

For the filling:

12 oz/300 g	cow's milk ricotta
⅜ cup/90 g	sugar
2	egg yolks
3½ tbsp/50 g	strong bread flour
2 tbsp/30 g	chocolate chips
3½ tbsp/50 g	candied orange peel
1 pinch	ground cinnamon

For many Italians, this ricotta cake, or *torta di ricotta*, has acquired true cult status. Delicate and not too sweet, with a flavor reminiscent of plain pastry tartlets, it is a very popular cake in Italy. The Neapolitans, for example, call it *pastiera* and are fond of adding refinements such as cereals, orange flower water or rosewater, and candied fruits. Children also enjoy eating this cake.

To make a good *torta di ricotta* it is important to thoroughly combine the ingredients for the cake mixture and filling. When preparing the cake dough it is essential to beat the butter and sugar together for a sufficiently long time before adding the other ingredients. Grate the lemon peel directly into the butter and sugar mixture.

The cream for the filling must be quite cool before it is folded into the ricotta. It should be cooled to room temperature and then refrigerated. In order to accelerate the cooling process, Paolo Luni spreads it on a marble slab.

Choose fresh, high-quality ricotta. This cream cheese is made from the whey obtained when the liquid is extracted from sheep's or cow's milk. The whey is reheated (*ricotta* means "cooked again") and the remaining liquid is gradually drained off. With its creamy consistency and acidic taste, ricotta is ideally suited to sweet dishes containing chocolate or candied fruits. Back in the 18th century, Antonio Frugoli, an Italian gourmet, advised using this delicious cheese when making cakes and doughnuts. Our chef recommends dissolving a little gelatin to brush the cake with when it has cooled after baking.

For the dough, place the sugar and softened butter, cut into pieces, in a bowl and knead thoroughly with the hands. Add 1 egg yolk, 2 whole eggs, the grated lemon peel, the inside of the vanilla pod, the flour, and the baking powder. Knead thoroughly and roll into a ball.

For the cream, heat the milk with the grated lemon peel. Combine the sugar, 2 egg yolks, and the flour in a saucepan until you have a golden-yellow mixture. Place the saucepan on the stove and pour in the milk and grated lemon peel. Cook for 10 minutes until thickened, stirring constantly. Chill for 1 hour.

For the filling, place the ricotta, sugar, 2 egg yolks, and flour in a bowl and stir. Carefully fold in the prepared cream.

Cake

Add the chocolate chips, finely chopped candied orange peel, and a pinch of cinnamon. Mix well.

Roll out the dough with a rolling pin into a circle ¼ in/4 mm thick and line a 10 in/ 25 cm baking pan with it. Cut off any dough above the top edge of the pan and set aside the remaining dough. Transfer the filling to the pastry case.

Roll out the remaining dough and cut into strips. Lay the strips on top of the filling in a lattice pattern and brush with egg yolk. Bake the cake in the oven for 40 minutes at 350° F/180° C. Leave to cool, then chill.

Almond

Preparation time: 30 minutes
Cooking time: 30 minutes
Difficulty: ★★

Serves 6

For the dough:
2 sticks/	
225 g	butter
⅞ cup/200 g	sugar
3	eggs
½	unwaxed lemon

½	vanilla pod
⅝ cup/100 g	strong bread flour

For the marzipan filling:
2½ cups/	
350 g	blanched almonds
3 scant cups/	
750 g	sugar
½	unwaxed lemon
½	vanilla pod
4	egg whites
4 oz/100 g	cookies (see below for recipe)

This almond cake is very common in the Veneto region and southern Lombardy. It is served at the end of a meal, often with a sparkling wine, and will keep without any problem for a week.

The chef recommends using strong bread flour to prepare the dough. This is suitable for cakes that are not meant to rise and results in a rather firm texture. For bread or *pannetone*, on the other hand, Paolo Luni uses superfine wheat flour, which makes yeast dough rise beautifully. To make it easier to roll out, dust the work surface with flour so the dough does not stick to it.

The principal filling for almond cake is marzipan. In the late Middle Ages, sugar was still unknown in Europe; it was first introduced from the Orient in the 11th century and remained a luxury until the Renaissance. At that time, sweet foods became more common, including marzipan,

which is still very popular today. The writer Bartolomeo Platina recorded a delicious marzipan recipe as long ago as the end of the 15th century.

The cookie crumbs lighten the filling and make it softer. You can easily make this cookie, which is very common in Italy: Combine 5 eggs and 2 egg whites with 1 scant cup/210 grams sugar, 2 cups/210 grams flour, and 3½ tablespoons/50 grams cornstarch. Bake the dough for 30 minutes at 350° F/180° C. Instead of this "Spanish bread," however, you can simply crumble ready-made plain dry cookies.

To garnish the cake, arrange blanched almonds in a pattern on top of the marzipan. When the cake is golden yellow, remove it from the baking pan and leave it to cool on a wire grid.

For the dough, knead 1¾ sticks/200 g soft butter and sugar with your hands. Add 2 whole eggs and 1 egg yolk, the grated lemon peel, inside of half a vanilla pod, and the flour.

Knead the dough thoroughly with the hands and roll into a ball. Using a rolling pin, roll out to a thickness of ¼ in/4 mm.

Wind the dough round the rolling pin and transfer to a buttered, floured 10 inch/ 25cm cake pan and set aside.

Cake

For the marzipan filling, combine 2 cups/ 300 g blanched almonds, the sugar, grated lemon peel, and inside of half a vanilla pod in a blender until the mixture resembles fine crumbs.

Add the egg whites and crumbled cookies and mix well with the marzipan filling.

Using your finger, make depressions in the dough all around the edge to form a garland pattern. Spread the marzipan filling evenly on top. Garnish with the remaining almonds. Bake for 30 minutes at 350° F/ 180° C. Remove from the baking pan immediately and cool on a wire grid.

The

Maddalena Beccaceci

Sauro Brunicardi

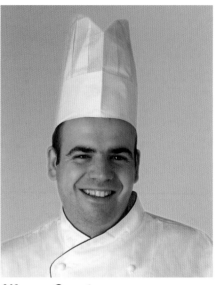

Alfonso Caputo

Francesca de Giovannini

Michelina Fischetti

Marco and Rossella Folicaldi

Chefs

Paolo Luni

Alberto Melagrana

Sergio Pais

Biancarosa Zecchin

Paolo Zoppolatti

Abbreviations:

1 oz = 1 ounce = 28 grams
1 lb = 1 pound = 16 ounces
1 cup = 8 ounces* (see below)
1 cup = 8 fluid ounces = 250 milliliters (liquids)
2 cups = 1 pint (liquids)
1 glass = 4–6 fluid ounces = 125–150 ml (liquids)
1 tbsp = 1 level tablespoon = 15-20 g* (see below) = 15 milliliters (liquids)
1 tsp = 1 level teaspoon = 3-5 g* (see below) = 5 ml (liquids)
1 kg = 1 kilogram = 1000 grams
1 g = 1 gram = $\frac{1}{1000}$ kilogram
1 l = 1 liter = 1000 milliliters = approx. 34 fluid ounces
1 ml = 1 milliliter = $\frac{1}{1000}$ liter

*The weight of dry ingredients varies significantly depending on the density factor, e.g. 1 cup flour weighs less than 1 cup butter.

Quantities in ingredients have been rounded up or down for convenience, where appropriate. Metric conversions may therefore not correspond exactly. It is important to use either American or metric measurements within a recipe.

© for the original edition: Fabien Bellahsen and Daniel Rouche
Execution and production: Fabien Bellahsen and Daniel Rouche
Photographs and technical direction: Didier Bizos
Photographic assistance: Morgane Favennec, Hasni Alamat
Editing: Élodie Bonnet, Nathalie Talhouas, with assistance from Elena Zapponi
Editorial assistance: Fabienne Ripon
Co-ordination: Marco Folicaldi

Original title: *Délices d'Italie*
ISBN of the original edition 2-84308-359-1
ISBN of the German edition 3-8331-2434-2

© 2006 for the English edition:
Tandem Verlag GmbH
KÖNEMANN is a trademark and an imprint of Tandem Verlag GmbH

Translation from German:
Judith Phillips for First Edition Translations Ltd, Cambridge, UK
Editor: Sally Heavens for First Edition Translations Ltd
Typesetting: The Write Idea in association with First Edition Translations Ltd
Project management: Mine Ali for First Edition Translations Ltd

Project Coordination: Isabel Weiler

Printed in Germany

ISBN 3-8331-2031-2

10 9 8 7 6 5 4 3 2 1
X IX VIII VII VI V IV III II I